Secret Bad Girl

A SEXUAL TRAUMA MEMOIR

AND RESOLUTION GUIDE

by Rachael Maddox

For J and all the Secret Bad Girls

Table of Contents

Prologue

SECRET BAD GIRL

I'm a secret and it's gotten bad
and all the reasons that I used to have
for keeping quiet, well, they've grown a mass
in the darkness of my hidden past

in the crevice of my private parts
where I wish that I could just restart
ain't there some kind of magic pill or curse
to undo all of the aching hurt?

'cuz I don't want
to be a secret no more
I just want
to be a good little girl
but there ain't no
traveling back in time
so I guess I'm

gonna have to find

my wildness
my lioness
my temptress
my Great Mother

my warrior
my servant's heart
my Redcloud love
my Great Father

too many secrets in our blessed world
we got brothels with 80 million girls
bein' sold off to the highest dime
while there's billions who don't have the time
to see, to see, to see

but we got lots of time
for Netflix binges
and shopping malls
and drunken brunches
and making sales
and Facebook quizzes
and Candy Crush
and rolling spliffs

and I'm sure that I do sound judgmental
but I've been the girl inside the brothel
and I've been the one to roll the spliff
and get real high

and say *gee-whiz*
what do we do now? what do we do now?
what do we do now? what do we do now?

'cuz we got these girls
who are tethered and splayed
yeah, we got these girls
who don't know what to say
and they'll act real tough
as their souls float away
but they need a mom, a mom
to look 'em in their eyes and say

find your wildness
your lioness
your temptress
your Great Mother

find your warrior
your servant's heart
your Redcloud love
your Great Father

find your endless rage
your fists of sage
your favorite way to say *gimmie more pleasure*

your yoga mat
your body fat
your most orgasmic lovely lover

your apologies
your eulogies
your sovereignty
your forgiveness

if you're a secret
and it's gotten bad
and all the reasons
that you used to have
for keeping quiet
well, they've grown a mass
in the darkness
of your hidden past
you can come clean
you can start to speak
you can even begin to sing
and that secret little girl within
she can grow
into a proud woman

Introduction

Dear Secret Bad Girl,

Once upon a time, we were all two year olds. I don't know about you, but I had short curly hair and an innocent mischief on my face. I was wild, full of wonder, and always up for a grocery store adventure. My mother dressed me in pink polka dot OshKosh B'Gosh overalls, which made it extra easy to feel like I could take on the world.

If you can, take a moment to picture yourself at this age, too. As you peek into that mental image of your younger self, can you see a bit of your most inherent nature? When you look with your mind's eye at the little one you used to be, what do you see?

For me at two years old, nothing quite dramatic or traumatic had happened in my life quite yet. However, it's possible that your story's a bit different, and the way you left the womb was less than pleasant. Maybe something scary happened when you were just a wee babe, or you came into a lineage that was wrought with pain and suffering, addiction or mistreatment.

Perhaps it would feel better to go back even farther than two years old in your mind's eye—back to the time before your official time began, when you were still just an idea in the ether, waiting to materialize, wanting—wanting to rain down as Human on this miraculous spinning disco ball called Earth.

There's a word in science called a *torus*, and it's used to describe that slippery slide moment that's just after you've been conceived, but just before you split into x and y cells. Leading edge mind-body therapists and many holistic health practitioners believe that in this magical moment, your entire natural blueprint of health, along with an inherent treatment plan (in case anything goes wrong), is created. And this natural blueprint of health is indestructible and incorruptible. Now, of course, *imprints* of life experience can form on top of or around this natural *blueprint*, making it seem as though the blueprint has disappeared, but still, nothing—not violence, violation, illness or abuse—can undo the deepest seedling of health that always lives within you.

I tell you all this, because if you choose to read this book, you'll be entering into the story of how I got lost inside a spell of violating imprints—imprints that convinced me I needed to hide in the secrecy of shame, that I must have been bad, crazy, slutty, stupid, broken, easily manipulated, destined for poverty, and most certainly beyond the reach of healing—otherwise, why? *why, why, WHY* would I have been so consistently and chronically *stuck*?

You'll *also* be entering into the story of how I circuitously found my way home to my blueprint: that wild, wondrous, innocent mischief at the core of my truest nature. My torus. My two year old. My grown ass woman who knows and loves her power. Who slings a ukulele over her shoulder and tours the nation with fervor. Who can have her lovers and her art, her yeses and her noes, her cash and her consciousness, her orgasms and her alone-time.

I went on many adventures to reclaim myself, worked with many kinds of healers, dedicated years and nearly every penny of my income at times to get the best help I could find. This is the wisdom I've mined from my adventures—the stories that live on for you.

Along with my stories, I've also included the Six Keys for Breaking the Trauma Spell, so that you can get started or continue along your own journey toward wonderful wholeness and health.

Before we dive in, I want to address that some of you may be wondering what qualifies me to write this book—to call myself a trauma "specialist"? It's true that I don't have a master's in psychology or a PhD in trauma resolution.

It's *also* true that I've read and highlighted seven books on trauma, front to back. It's *also* true that I've worked with one of the world's best trauma resolution practitioners, as well as many incredible shamans and coaches to bring resolution to my own trauma. It's *also* true that I have a lived and felt sense of the way trauma grabs hold of the nervous system and builds stories and emergencies on top of it, and how, with proper attention and guidance, the body can be restored to regulation, vitality and power. From my perspective, my insatiable passion, personal experience, and devotion to learning and practicing as much as I can, qualify me as a "specialist". But you are most certainly welcome to decide for yourself.

Before the story begins, I feel compelled to offer you a very important wish. It's a bit of a strange wish for an author to offer her readers, but that's ever more reason for offering it.

My wish for you is this: *as you read through the pages of this book, please respect your physiology.*

I share stories that are quite intense and potentially triggering. I don't harp on those stories, in particular, but still—just reading them could possibly activate a trauma-doused nervous system. Reading slowly and taking note of what's happening in your body, gives you the opportunity to *choose*. Choose to stay and keep reading, or choose put the book down and do something more soothing.

You have the choice to stay or to go. Always. Here, and everywhere.

The following questions may help you make the most empowering choice:

Are you feeling hot? Sweaty? Angry? Sad? Numb?

Are you spinning at all in your mind?

Are you reading lines, but not knowing what they're saying?

If any of these things begin happening, put the book down for a moment, feel your body's contact with the ground below you, and inquire if you truly want to keep reading, or not.

I care more that you move at a pace that respects your physiology, than finish this book. After all, respecting your body's boundaries is the heart of trauma resolution.

No need to push anything in.

Deal?

Last, I want you to know why I'm sharing my most intimate stories—stories that could potentially trigger or offend—when I could simply write the science, the facts, the tools at face value.

Here's why: I, personally, find myself more inside of stories than facts. I can relate to sisterhood more than stoic diagnosis. And perhaps you're like me. Perhaps you may not ever realize you're living under a trauma spell unless someone else's story looks a whole lot like yours, and they're brave enough to tell it, and you're brave enough to listen.

So here we are. I am telling you everything. The magic. The mess up's. The scandals. The revelations. Because I want you to walk through the world knowing and asserting your boundaries, trusting and expressing your creativity, feeling worthy of money and fulfilling relationships, enjoying sex, having clarity and confidence, taking good care of your health. And I want you to know that you're not bad or alone if these things feel secretly impossible and the reason why feels terribly hidden.

If you're coming to this book trauma-free, simply curious about the way sexual trauma may look or feel, work or unwind, please know that I don't share the details of my expletives in vein or to be exhibitionistic. If you can withhold judgment about the details, and instead, look for the patterns and causes (which I do my best to tease out), you'll find the understanding you're looking for. You'll also become part of a movement to recognize, de-stigmatize and unshame the ways trauma can influence behavior.

Back to you, Secret Bad Girl. Here's what I want you to know: you are so much more than the imprints of violation you've experienced. You are an unbreakable blueprint of health and goodness, power and resilience. You deserve to experience your wholeness. And you can. Even if it feels so far fetched right now. My great hope is that this book will help you see what's possible, and guide you closer and closer home to your most magical lovable core.

Endless love,
Rachael

P.S.—Not 100% sure if you're a Secret Bad Girl, and really wanting to know? Feel free to head to the book website for a short quiz before you read on: www.secret-badgirlfreebies.com.

P.P.S.—In the forward to Soul Craft by Bill Plotkin, he invites the reader to read each poem at the beginning of the chapter out loud, two times over. I loved this practice while reading his book, and would invite you to do the same. Something changes, in a cellular kind of way, when we let words slowly move through us and leave our lips.

Part 1

LIES

trauma lies
at the base of my
spine
sputtering
bad
bad
bad
girl

Chapter 1

THE IMPRINT

Picture a girl. Five years old. Soft curly golden hair and the cutest plum cheeks on earth. She lives in a relatively "good" home with plenty of money for the things that matter. Two parents. An older brother. She's enrolled in a scrimmage soccer league and feels safe to rake piles and jump into the autumn leaves. She's happy. And wild. And free. And five.

On some days, with all that wild freedom, she has play dates with her friend Jessica and they secretly tip-toe into the hidden corner behind the plaid couch in the basement den. This—this is when the Secret Bad Girl comes out. The one who asks her other Secret Bad Girl friend, "Do you want to play The Game?" And their eyes widen and they giggle quietly as they slip off their pink Umbro t-shirts and hug their flat chested bare-breasted bodies into each others' innocent mysteries. They kiss like woodpeckers on trees. They agree to take off their panties and then giggle more at their nudity. When her Mom hollers down from the top of the stairs, they freeze and jolt for their underwear. Game over, Secret Bad Girls.

Picture a girl. Eight Years old. At night, her parents fight—slam doors, throw curse words, leave the television on as a buffer 'til the morn. Her brother hides, but she— she tries to find ways to make everyone get along. She cries, counsels and begs, and when none of that works, she makes up hopeful love songs to save her own sense of honor. *She wants*. She wants love in the air. Attention. Care. She wants to feel herself getting somewhere with all her valiant effort to make the fighting better. But no matter her might, she can't seem to wage peace in this home. Plain and simple: she's bad at it.

Picture a girl. 11 years old. Double chinned and anything but thin, even though she runs the track thrice weekly. Boy crazy and wishing there was a way she could fool them into liking her, she practices her kissy face nightly in the mirror. When that doesn't work, she tries to be funny. When *that* doesn't work, she thinks, *maybe I should try that thing I've heard of... slutty?*

Picture a girl. 13 years old. Thinned out, but still thinking she must be fat. Still feeling the ache of wishing her home felt more like romance than an emotional war zone. Still trying to fill that hole of holy love. She's 13 now, so maybe she's not exactly a girl. Her parents brag to their friends that she's 13 going on 30, and she can't help but agree, as she plays the role of family shrink and thinks she's the only sane one in the household.

Picture this know-it-all sitting in the computer room

downstairs, legs slung over the side of a chair, face glowing in the humming screen light. Her parents are watching television in the other room. Her brother's playing video games. She signs onto Instant Messenger. She jumps in with her good friend Heather.

Heather's having sex with someone who's 27. He's a family-friend of sorts. A guy coming from a trusted source. A curious but safe enough person that her parents regularly let her hang with him without pausing to wonder what's happening. The know-it-all girl thinks it's exciting and strange and wonderful and perhaps a *little* deranged, but mostly very exciting.

Tell me the latest, Heather!, she types.

Heather responds, typing faster, faster, faster. About how good it feels to have him lick her. About how strangely great it is when he butt fucks her. About the unbelievable truth that he really loves her. He really, *really* loves her.

The girl confirms, *That's great! I'm really, really happy for you.*

Secretly, her insides feel strange—especially about the anal sex stuff—but no, *this is her friend Heather! This is exciting! This is just for fun! What could be so bad about this?*

So when Heather asks the girl if she'd ever want to have a threesome with her 27-year-old secret boyfriend… *Maybe he'd let you take it from behind… we could do it together. It'll be fuuuuun!…* the girl cringes inside and stutters.

Uhhhh… but I've never done this before.

Uhhhh… but how will my parents let me out the

door?

Uhhhh… but isn't he yours?

--I never had either… it's great!

--We can tell them we're going on a movie friend-date!

--There's plenty of fun for the two of us!

Picture a girl slipping on a small red thong with pink elastic straps and glittery lips on front. Picture her pulling up ass-tight white capris, a low-cut black tee, and lacing on some clean white sneaks. Picture her rounding her eyes with thick black lines, accentuating her lips with soft shiny pink, de-frizzing her curls with sticky gel and spraying her body with a too-sweet citrus smell.

Picture a girl twirling a finger through her hair, standing between her parents and their blaring television obsession, asking a simple question.

Can I go to the movies at 7 with Heather?

--Who's driving?

Her friend James.

--It's okay with us, if it's okay with her parents.

Picture a girl skipping out the front door, *Bye, guys! See you later!*; stuffing her sneaky feeling down low, making sure that nobody knows that anything could possibly be bad here.

Picture a small black Honda Civic, Heather grinning from the passenger seat of it, the girl slipping deep into the back leather seats, already regretting what she'd gotten herself into.

Picture a 30-minute drive with music on blast, fog shimmering off the black asphalt whizzing by. Picture pulling into a motel on the side of a dingy road in an area of town the girl knew of as downtrodden and dangerous. Picture her waiting in the car with Heather and then being called into the lobby as an Indian man makes her sign some kind of waiver she isn't so sure about.

Picture her walking up wet stairs to the second floor of the motel where she waits outside the door as James jiggles the key in the lock. Picture her standing at the side of the bed thinking, *Now what?*

Picture smells she'll never forget and feelings of wet that confuse her. Picture her watching her friends' eyes watching her. Picture her leaving her body, thinking she's deceiving herself, as he holds her hands down and squeezes his penis into her anus. Picture her knowing that time had passed without knowing much else of what happened. Picture her going to the bathroom, pulling the forest green silk robe off the back of the door coat hanger, wrapping it around her scared Bad Girl body, closing the lid to the toilet, sitting atop it, and calling her friend Jennifer Simms—chatting as if nothing has happened.

Picture a girl who acts like nothing has happened for four whole years until she's a senior in high school and can't stop secretly hating Heather. Until she breaks down and tells her two best friends (who are shocked but don't know what to do), and her mom (who almost instantaneously "forgets" that she's told her).

Picture a girl who then goes on to fill out the archetype of Secret Bad Girl over and over again. As if her brain had been imprinted with a covert badge. (Because it had.) As if the neural-pathways toward self-destructive behavior cleared wider, while the ones leading towards self-confidence and authentic empowerment narrowed.

(Because they had.)

Picture a girl who *doesn't know* that her brain and nervous system are living under a trauma spell. A girl who's secretly blaming herself for all the secret bad things she's done and all the secret ways she's stuck in a haze of low self-worth.

They say that when a brain's been traumatized, bad things stick to it like Velcro, and good things roll off of it like Teflon.

In this Secret Bad Girl's case:

Velcro: anonymous blowjobs.

Teflon: emotionally safe boyfriends.

Velcro: secret affairs with people twice her age.

Teflon: a deep confidence that she could give and get the love she deserved.

Velcro: a deluge of self-blaming and self-shaming thoughts.

Teflon: boundaries, righteousness, sovereignty, self-love.

Velcro: YES, I'll do that thing that insults my body and soul.

Teflon: no thanks, mister.

Velcro: giving away her greatest work for free.

Teflon: money.

Velcro: marijuana to numb the trauma.

Teflon: presence and resilience amidst intensity.

Like most people who have bad things sticking to them like Velcro, this Secret Bad Girl began to espouse the dark belief that *she must be bad*. Or stupid. Or to blame. Or broken. Or beyond help.

This was a logical conclusion. She'd been trying really

hard to make better choices, and experienced minimal success. So why wouldn't she think she's bad?

It wasn't only logical, it was also *possible*. Possible that this Secret Bad Girl (and other people who have bad things sticking to them like Velcro) was addicted to pain, got a rise out of risky adventures, was on a mission to stay poor, or just didn't want to do the work of loving herself better. It was possible that people were trying to help her, and still, she moved towards the not-so-good kind of mischief.

But in reality? The truth was somewhere in the middle.

I know because, as you may have guessed by now, the story of this Secret Bad Girl is mine. I did (and still do) like adventures. I was probably partially addicted to pain, but not because it was "true to my nature," but rather because it was imprinted all around me. I took all the help I could get, gladly, and very much wanted to love myself better. But still, in the most private sacred corners of my life, my choices often looked much more self-hating and hopeless.

My question is, Why? Why would I or you or anyone else *choose* the Secret Bad Girl life? Choose the Velcro? Choose the shitty love or the crude lack of connection? The shame of giving yourself away in the most inauthentic ways?

It's certainly not because those things *feel good*, provide a sense of safety, or get anyone closer to their dream lives. So why? Why the spiraling? Why the continuation of "choosing bad"? Why the stickiness?

So often in the self-help world, we're told it's because

we don't love ourselves.

But I've learned there's another version to the story—one I could only see once the trauma spell loosened its grip on me. Perhaps all these "choices" were not as much of a "choice" as they seemed.

Throughout most of my time as a Secret Bad Girl, I tried tirelessly to "make better choices". I later learned that with traumatic imprints on board, I was living mostly in hyperactive and hypoactive states of fear, and my decisions were hijacked by a warped *physiology*. My choices were a reflection of a life-or-death fear adrenaline that was stuck in me, hung over from past experiences that rattled me to my core more than I ever realized.

Of course, I still had that know-it-all 13-year-old personality inside, so I did *not* want to believe that anything could possibly be "wrong" with me. *I can figure this out on my own*, I thought. *I can get out of this mess by myself.* And sure—while, ultimately, I did find the right healers to help me, I spent so much time trying and trying with my *mind* to resolve what was ultimately a misalignment of my physiology and warped imprinting on my spirit.

In the end, that 13-year-old was right. There was and is nothing wrong with me. My natural blueprint of health was always there, underneath all the Velcro of my traumatic imprints.

And yet, she was also wrong. I couldn't get out of the mess alone, because the nature of the mess—the true cause of it—was a secret to me. I had no way of seeing myself as traumatized.

No one talks about trauma. I knew nothing about its true nature. I didn't know that when something violating happens, it can get stuck in your body like a violation hangover, and last for months, years, decades or a whole lifetime. I didn't know that this violation hangover was hiding beyond my conscious awareness. I didn't know that there were physiological reasons why I was repeating self-destructive patterns over and over again.

I just thought that I was fucked up and made bad choices. I just thought that if anyone knew what I'd done, *they'd* think I was fucked up and made bad choices. I didn't think there was help for the kind of problem I had. Because I didn't even understand that the kind of problem I had was anything other than shameful.

I also had no sight for connecting the dots. I didn't understand that the violation hangover of trauma was affecting more than just my sex life, but my whole life. I didn't see how the *energies* of the particular violation I experienced—manipulation, coercion, secrecy and shame—were the same energies that were most destructive in my life on all fronts. They were the same energies that kept me small in my expression or covert with my addictions. The ones that kept me easily taken advantage of and secretly feeling worthless.

Also, let's not forget that even if I could have considered myself traumatized (which I couldn't have, really) I was straight up terrified to go into the pain of it all. Which is something exceptionally common and scientifically sound when you're living with trauma.

The body and subconscious knows that it will get activated when it readdresses an old trauma. Which is why the body and subconscious will often keep you very far away from the things that might help you heal—because the things that might help you heal often require you to face the beast.

For a very long time, my body and subconscious knew that I was not ready to face my trauma. And I say "ready" very intentionally. Because in the same way that every human body has a natural blueprint of health—every human body also has an inherent treatment plan for healing after things have gone awry. That treatment plan often includes lots of time away from the pain, simply waiting until the conditions are correct—safe and loving and supportive enough—for dealing with the descent and rise of deep healing.

For years there was no one on earth who I wanted to show just how strong the shadows of my rage and grief could get. Not even myself. So, of course, I blocked that idea from my mental realm of possibility, and went on spiraling like any good Secret Bad Girl would.

What I know now is that my choices during that decade of Secret Bad Girl living were a reflection of my physiology that was still wired for violation. I could try to *will* my physiology to respond differently, but my choices wouldn't truly change until I learned how to shed traumatic imprints at the most foundational physical and energetic levels.

And the surprisingly good news about it all?

Facing the beast of my trauma looked a whole lot different than how I thought it would. My rage and my grief, my shame and my fear—they were taken care of by my body. My body knew how to move them up and out far better than my mind ever could have.

I didn't have to struggle inside the re-telling of my

story to experience tremendous healing. I didn't have to mentally pound things into perfectly healthy placement.

With the care and guidance of a somatic trauma therapist, my body was empowered to reclaim herself. And this is the miracle I wish I could tell the whole wide world: *your body can heal your mind.*

Let's back up, though. Go back to the story. Zoom in on you.

Maybe your story sounds similar to mine, or perhaps a tad bit different. Maybe in yours, you're the "Heather"—roping others in to your secret attempts to feel loved or safe inside a big pit of trouble. Maybe your parents or religious upbringing had an extremely repressive opinion about sexuality, and everything you did had to be sneaked. Maybe you got caught red handed in a forbidden act and smacked across the face, called a slut. Maybe everyone thought you were really, really good, but you were having emotionally unsafe sex with your perfectly friendly boyfriend, and it began to affect everything without your conscious cognition.

Maybe you secretly disdain yourself for all of this, and also secretly have no clue where to go or what to do. Or maybe you're older now, have gone to a good therapist, and know what you're supposed to believe about yourself. (Maybe you even believe it!) Maybe you've done some big hearty healing. Maybe you're on your way to breathing differently. And yet—sex or cash or confidence still never seems to go as planned.

As you read this book, Secret Bad Girl, I want you to hold the possibility that there may be another version of your story that you don't know yet. Yes—it's possible that you *did* fuck up, that you *did* manipulate, that you *have been* weak or slutty or in love with hurting yourself or addicted to low self worth. That's what I thought was true for me.

But what I also came to discover over 10 years of struggling and then finally emerging on the other side, is that I wasn't as bad as I thought. I was actually under a trauma spell from the very start. From the moment I learned to be afraid of my wildness, my hot faced wonder, my innocent love for discovering the sensual and the ecstatic—from that moment on I was creating realities that aligned with my traumatized physiology. We all are. We all do.

Every single Secret Bad Girl has learned her cues for shut down, has followed those directions until she makes no sounds of authentic confidence or deep self-reliance. She's been hollowed out and turned around—screwed from behind and made to define herself on how good she can seem on the outside. This is the hallmark of a Secret Bad Girl. *It's hard to tell she's in there.*

Dearest Secret Bad Girl, I know it's horrible. I know it seems impossible to change. I know there's a way that you'd rather stay in a cycle of self-blame or know-it-all illusion or it's-too-expensive confusion so you never have to become all the way awake, feel all your rage, all your power, all your pleasure. I know the rape culture culprit feels too big to fight or prison. But I'm telling you, we can win this thing. Together, we can break the spell. But first, it may help if you know how I came to see the spell for myself. How I started to be able to tell that I wasn't actually *bad*. How the lie I was living under began to slowly unravel.

NO

i've kept this two letter secret for so long--
in the submission of my cooperative lungs
the sweet scrunched ponytail of my youthful throat
the back of my ever-swallowing tonsils
and tips of my agreeable taste buds--
that i can't help but wonder
what tumors grow in the silence of truth

Chapter 2

THE SURRENDER

SAVED BY SEXLESSNESS

My first semester of college, I moved into the dorms a week early to take part in a community service project. Secret Bad Girl intact, I managed to meet a cute Sophomore at the dining hall on my very first night on campus, go back to his dorm, and give him a blow job.

A few days later, I met another guy, this time with a totally different vibe—wavy hair, a plaid shirt and dirty red chucks, playing wiffle ball with a group of friends. This guy's name was Brian, and there would be no introductory blow jobs. Just high fives and goofy laughs.

Brian and I quickly became friends over shared political beliefs and a knack for actually listening. There was clear emotional interest between us, and yet, no sexual moves were being made. Naturally, my inner Secret Bad

Girl found this very unusual.

It took five whole hangouts before we finally kissed. That night, we laid under a living-room-sized fort, knee to knee, talking sweetly, until he whispered to me, "Can I ask you a question?" and I thought, *Good god, I thought he'd never kiss me.* Upon which he asked, "Do you want to go on a date *next* Friday?" It was Saturday. I was DYING. *Is this man going to wait until an official first date to kiss me?*

Enter: bad-girl-with-good-guy-confusion-paralysis. It looks like this: a sweet man takes his time getting to know a generally promiscuous girl. He lays down no moves and asks for no immediate blow jobs. All the girl can think is, *What the fuck is happening here?*

About twenty minutes later he chimed back in, "Can I ask you another question?" *YES YES YES,* I moaned silently. "Can I give you a little kiss?"

We kissed tenderly and lovingly, softly and sweetly. And something about the wholesome holiness of it all had butterflies pirouetting in my belly until the sun came up outside his double-paned windows. Two weeks later, I plopped onto the bottom bunk of my roommate's bed, called up my oldest childhood friend Micayla, and whispered, "I know this sounds crazy, but I'm going to marry this guy." We both squealed like little girls.

Brian was a virgin when we met, and also straight edge. I, on the other hand—well, you know a bit of my history. Meeting Brian was like having a fiery Arian angel fall from the sky, sent direct from God, to keep me safe and dignified during the vulnerable ride of college debauchery and mayhem. Luckily, in college, there would be little mayhem for me. Instead, I got a return to innocence.

The first time Brian and I had sex I cried all night long. The sex had been mild. Unaggressive. Nice. Dare I say… boring. The kissing was beautiful and the love was palatable—but still. I was mortified. Sitting up in his twin bed, streetlight flooding in through the blinds, my mind raced with worry. *Do love and sex not go together? Will I always want something more aggressive because of the way this whole journey started for me? This was the nicest sex I've ever had—why do I feel so disappointed?*

The Secret Bad Girl in me felt orphaned and silenced. After all, she'd just won the Good lottery, and Bad had proven quite dangerous. *Don't fuck it up now,* she thought. *Don't try to get more or different. Just keep quiet. Just make this work.*

WHEN SECRET MEMORIES BECOME REAL AGAIN

Fast-forward six years. The sex got more interesting, and Brian and I, feeling solid and in love, got hungry for a big adventure. We decided to get married and bike around the country as an extended honeymoon. On April 1st, 2011—Brian's 24th birthday—we left from the steps of our 8-person vegan cooperative in DC.

It was 45 degrees and rainy. (The weather was a foreboding sign of the mood to come on our adventure.)

The first 10 days of the trip we traveled from DC to Pittsburg on the C&O Canal tow-path. This was supposed to be a quite "seamless" portion of our ride since it was a straight shot on a trail with no cars interfering or directions needed. However, incessant rain turned the tow-path to heavy mud, and the already bumpy trail became almost violently so.

Cue: lots of thumping and thudding of my bike seat against my vagina.

Cue: 10 days of flashbacks. To that time in the motel room. To that time in the guy's backyard. To that time in the back seat of Jeff's Jeep, parked in the mall parking lot. To that time in the back seat of Jordan's SUV, parked in the movie theatre parking lot.

"Brian... Are you thinking about anything... intense?"

"Uh... Nope! Why, what's up?"

"Oh... uh. Nothing."

Cue: the awakening of my dormant sexual trauma.

The physical stress, directed in the exact place where my memories were laced with *Bad*, was too much to push aside or override. But again—I just thought something was wrong with me. That I was being what we like to call "emo". That I needed to tough it up, suck it up, and just keep going. That it was okay to override my body's limits. That it was my duty as a good wife to simply deal with it.

For 8 months I kept going. At the edge of my physical limits, I pedaled and sweat and climbed mountains and pissed in bushes and used a rubber saddle bag stuffed with clothes as my pillow and the boney earth as my bed. For *my* physiology—a physiology already torqued and pressurized by unresolved memories—this meant I was travelling closer and closer to a total nervous system break down.

Of course, I didn't know this. I knew nothing about trauma. I just knew that I'd had those flashbacks at the beginning of the trip, that I had ZERO interest in sex with my husband, and that I was completely exhausted the entire trip. But I was riding a bike across the country. Who wouldn't be exhausted?

We got home after 8 months of adventuring, and my withering continued. For a week, I could barely move. I laid on a mattress on the floor of my good friend Jen's attic, stared out the window and watched as the neighbors across the street cut down a fifty-year-old tree. I remember weeping that day, thinking I was carrying something old and dead in me, but not really understanding what or how.

Then, a month had passed, and I still felt completely lifeless.

I lovingly refer to Jen as my "old lady friend" even though she's only twenty years older. I call her that because she's wise—and I don't use that word lightly. She knows the right things to say when people die or feel lost or fried or have no clue why they're still tired after sleeping for 30 days straight.

Jen took us in to her home and her family. Told us we could stay as long as we needed. Asked nothing in return but for some help with the groceries. So when 30 days had passed, and I was still lying on the mattress in the attic, concerned, Jen made me little scrolls of paper with the simplest instructions inside them. "Take a shower." "Call Jodi." "Eat an orange." "Read some poetry."

"All you have to do," she told me, "is pull one of these scrolls each day and do what it says. Nothing more."

The simplest things felt excruciatingly hard. But I followed my old lady friend's instructions, and eventually, day-by-day, bits of life came back into my body.

On the Brian front, things were rocky. We'd done something incredibly challenging and incredibly beautiful together—but had very different experiences of it. He got home full of life and excitement. I got home with a body full of activated trauma and a hard-to-understand depression.

Simultaneously, the Occupy movement had taken foot, and Brian, an avid activist, attended almost-daily meetings and protests after getting off work at the bike shop. He wanted my presence there, but I couldn't bear the crowds or the cold. For month after month, he'd leave the house early and come home quite late. We went from seeing each other 24-7 for eight months straight, to hardly at all.

Meanwhile, at home, I was having backroom conversations about polyamory with people on the Internet. It seemed like an interesting concept to me, and as my body was waking up more and more, so was my sex drive.

One day, Brian came home, and I said to him, "Bri, you're dating socialism. How would you feel about me dating other people—you know, without breaking up?"

In the end, it wasn't quite that simple. We *did* both date other people, but our awakenings through that process ended up loosening the knot we'd tied to each other, and in turn, roused the realization that we wanted to go our separate ways. Looking back, it's clear that we needed *some* kind of doorway out, and opening our relationship served as a mostly peaceful one. We'd loved each other so much and so well, that without something to loosen the knot we'd tied, we probably would've stayed with each other to the detriment of our happiness and our growth.

But just because it was right to split, didn't mean it was easy.

WELCOME BACK, SECRET BAD GIRL

With my husband gone, almost 8 years of safety and cuddles was no longer protecting me—in life, with the bills, and most certainly not in the bedroom.

I was 25 and single for the first time as an adult.

The first guy I dated was my Bikram instructor. (In secrecy, naturally.) He was 20 years older than me, a master of the body, and had me ejaculating on the side of the road in the front seat of his gray Jeep Cherokee the first time we ever hooked up. I was… hooked. Things were fun and exciting for about a month until he refused to kiss me while we were having sex, claiming that it was "just a problem *he* was having, not something that should affect *me*." Never mind that *I* was there… letting him put his dick in my vagina.

Then Jen set me up with someone she'd gone on a date with, thinking sparks might fly between us. Let's just call this guy Matt. Our first date, which was more than a bit alcohol laced, ended with hot and heavy making out in the front seat of his car. On our second date, I went to Matt's house, got high, and got raped so hard I was left physically wordless for a week.

That's when I started thinking that maybe I was seriously broken. That maybe I should deal with my Secret

Bad Girl problem, which had returned with a violent vengeance.

I thought of getting help, but help was scary. I didn't want to tell my slutty secrets. I'd been living inside them for so long, that they felt mute and ironed into me—like body parts that couldn't be severed or handed over to someone else for examination. No, my secrets were stuck inside the crevice of my uterus, buried deep beyond the tunnel of my vagina. They would require bait, hooks, fishing out.

WHEN THE SECRET GETS FISHED OUT

Living back in DC in a new group house, I picked up a job at an indie café to get by. One of my co-workers, a tall and doggish looking guy named Owen, was there to bring in some extra cash while he was finishing up acupuncture school. For months, he tried to get me to come in for a session—become one of his practicum clients. Finally, our schedules aligned, and I said yes.

Sitting with a pen and clipboard at Tai Sophia Acupuncture School, I went through my physical history on a checklist. Normal questions about family medical history, injuries, medications. And then. "Have you ever experienced rape or sexual violence? If so, please write when and what."

I was stopped dead in my tracks. Blood to my feet. Mind clearing out. But despite my shameful secrecy, part of me still wanted it to be known. Part of me still quietly hoped I could be helped. I scribbled, *Yes. Anal statutory rape. 13. Date rape. 25. Twice.*

When Owen and I reviewed my history, he did something no one had ever done before. He asked if I'd ever gotten professional help for my rapes. As a coach, someone in the healing arts, I felt significantly embarrassed that my answer was *no*. So I told him the best truth I could find that also slightly saved face. "Well… I'm going to an all women's circus camp! It's supposed to be all about healing and empowerment. I think that's gonna really help."

He nodded compassionately, and in a very doctorly way, simply re-stated his stance. "You know, you can get professional help for this. I'd like to encourage you to do that."

"I will. Promise."

THE BACKDOOR INTO HEALING

I was on the Oregon Coast for my best friend's birthday and I had this insatiable feeling, kept saying this phrase, "There are not enough cartwheels in the WORLD for this body." My body wanted to wake up. Badly.

I Google searched "adult circus camp". Three items down was WiseFool New Mexico—a radical circus school focused on social justice and personal empowerment. The tag line for their all-women circus intensive? *Transformation through the circus arts*. "A place for women to explore their physical and inner strength while building trust and community." *This!*, I thought. *Maybe I could just do this to get the help I need, and not have to deal with my trauma directly.*

So I up and moved to Santa Fe for 6 weeks of circus play that loosened all the cracks and crevices in me. The instructors of BUST were all healers (and badasses)—some explicitly, some inherently. It was perfect sisterhood embodiment medicine. Difficult. Difficult to let myself play. To feel my body so alive and still somehow so tired. But amazing, like coming home to my true nature.

As the fates would have it, I was sent to live with a woman who was dying of cancer. That woman took me with her to a very intense soul retrieval therapy session, where it came out that she and her sister had both been molested as kids. I was there as her "support person", but ended up going into my own deep recessive depression just from hearing her story. I slept for two weeks straight, but when I finally awoke, I had my own soul retrieval session. The first bit of a promise kept.

But my experience of soul retrieval was exhausting. I cried four whole buckets in one day, and without any kind of ongoing follow up support, I just felt raw and tired. I got home and decided it'd be better if I just continued with life as usual.

I met many men. Had sex with many men. A few women, too. There was John Very Handsome, and John the musician. Megan #1 and Megan #2. There was Dennis the filmmaker skydiver. There was Brett the polyamorous dude who I found annoying, but had sex with anyway. There was the "tornado sex guy" I met at a bar whose name I've conveniently forgotten.

By the time I was having sex with Brett, I'd also moved out to Portland, Oregon where Jodi was living. In Portland, it seemed like every person alive was a broke polyamorous healer in a band. I fit the bill—minus the poly part—but I played along to make things easier. Brett and I would have six-hour sex marathons and I'd feel empty inside for three days following. Still. *Maybe these juices can fill me up,* I'd think.

I went in and out of cycles of celibacy since the loveless sex spurts left me feeling excruciatingly empty. I went back and forth between regular acupuncture and regular dance. I wrote morbid poems. I lit candles and prayed. But still. I did not seek professional help. After all, I was being bad. I had gotten myself into this mess. I was broke. I was definitely to blame. And there was no real way to resolve what I was doing anyway, since if there had been, I would've been able to figure it out on my own, smart girl that I am.

SECRET PULSING PAIN

It started as just a nagging feeling in my right vulva. I thought maybe I had an STD. Brett called me and told me he had syphilis, and that I probably gave it to him since he'd used protection with all his other partners. I got tested at Planned Parenthood. Clear. No STDs. No notable problems. No explanation for the pain.

The nag turned into torment. I started going to community acupuncture two or three times a week for the pain. My acupuncturist, Allyndreth, put me on Chinese herbs that helped some, but when my first period came after starting the herbs, I turned ghost white and passed out convulsing in the shower. My housemate rushed me to the office that was just down the street, and Allyndreth and her marvelous assistant midwifed me through what had all the symptoms of a miscarriage, with none of the science. (At the time, I'd been celibate for many months.) I passed the largest blood clots of my life and then passed out for nearly 48 hours.

There were days I couldn't walk, the pain so intense. I'd cry and cry and call Jodi and pray and smoke pot to numb the pain. I'd try to get off, even though it hurt like hell, thinking maybe if I could just inject some pleasure into this place of so much pain, maybe then, it would finally go away. It did not go away.

SECRET CANCER SCARE

According to holistic health, up and out is better than down and in.

Jodi moved to Florida, and with my housing arrangement up and the dark Portland winter dragging on, I decided I'd go join her. I left most of my belongings in storage in a friend's basement figuring I'd be back, packed a few suitcases for the sunshine, and was off.

On the day before my 28th birthday, I met a Cuban musician with wild curly hair like mine at the bar on the beach in Fort Lauderdale. I asked him if he wanted to trade songs the next day, as a birthday celebration of sorts. He said of course, and that he'd bring the mimosas and pot. *"Anything else you'd like, darling?"* Our song share escalated into a private-parts share (on par with everyone's expectations) and the next day, I was checkin' myself out in the mirror, when I noticed a large purple-red spot on my vulva.

I went to Planned Parenthood where they told me I

had all the symptoms of vaginal melanoma. Long-story short, it was atypia (a step away from melanoma), but with the chances of it developing into melanoma at nearly 100%, three different doctors recommended that I have it surgically removed.

I did all the things they tell you not to do about researching medical conditions online, and terrified, drove through an uncharacteristic ice storm in the Carolinas all the way home to my parents' house in Maryland.

Added to my Bad Girl shame was the warning my dad had given me over and over again: "If anything ever happens to you and you can't take care of yourself because you don't have any money, we're not going to be able to help you, Rachael. We're not going to be able to help." Of course, his warning came from his own version of love, his deep desire for me to really get on my own two feet financially.

But I didn't know how to tell my dad that I was on a secret epic healing adventure that would cost me my twenties but grant me my power. I didn't know how to tell him, because I wasn't sure it was true.

Nevertheless, when I called from the car and told my parents what was going on, crying with fear that I couldn't actually come home, that they wouldn't be able to help me—my mom scolded my father in shouts full of love for her daughter, and insisted that I come home— now.

I had a marble-sized chunk of my vulva removed by a kind man named Dr. Grace. (The synchronicity wasn't lost on me.) The pain was excruciating for a good two months, and my brain chemistry was seriously destroyed from having so much of my pleasure-circuit sending emergency signals to my brain.

Cue: my second round of major trauma flashbacks.

Cue: a two-week bender of weed, whisky and narcolepsy in my childhood bedroom, with my parents down the hall.

I wrote a few good songs. I FaceTimed with my friends on the west coast. I meditated on dying. I tried to force myself to masturbate even though I could only feel pain. (Again.)

I was utterly non-functional and needed serious and immediate help. But trapped in a trauma spell and embarrassed to be home with my parents at 28, my system was insistent on going back and forth between fight, flight and freeze—none of which encouraged me to stay where I was and get suitable, professional help.

I pushed myself to move back to Portland where work was waiting for me.

I told myself I'd deal with "it"—the madness of my unresolved trauma—when I got there.

I didn't have to.

"It" dealt with me.

SECRET SOUL CONTRARIAN

Caroline Myss has this theory that in the same way we have soul "mates", we also have soul "contrarians"— people that help awaken our destinies through presenting opposition or difficulty, which then gives us the opportunity to stretch, grow and overcome.

One night back in Portland, I was feeling especially

rattled from a simple conflict in my new workplace. (With activated trauma, little bumps can become monstrous mountains.) Knowing my vulnerable condition and my specific history of sexual trauma, my mentor-boss offered to take me to her boyfriend's for dinner as an offering of comfort and care.

That night was anything but comforting or caring. Strange and inappropriate sexual passes were made at me and explicit sexual behavior was conducted in front of me—by my boss and her boyfriend.

Cue: a very unexpected soul contrarian.

At that point, I didn't have the time, energy or mental capacity to respond reasonably or call for help. I simply dissociated. Disappeared. Disintegrated into white fairy dust where nothing could cut another centimeter down.

They dropped me off in the morning, at which point I finally began to awaken a bit from my dissociative stupor, *at which point* a deluge of tears came that lasted for three full days.

I'd wake up in the morning, crying uncontrollably. I'd call my mom. I'd call Jen. I'd call Jodi. *What's wrong with me? I can't stop crying. I feel like I'm inside an impossibly large black hole. I don't know where I am.*

"Are you scared of something, Rachael?" my mom asked. I told her what happened with my mentor-boss. "That's not professional, Rachael. Not at all."

I told Jen what happened. "You need to come home, Rachael. You have to get away from her, now. You need to assert that you can protect yourself."

I told Jodi what happened. "It sounds like you need your mom, Rach."

Cue: the opportunity to stretch, grow and overcome.

I'd only moved back to Portland two weeks prior, but within 48 hours, in a state of total disarray, calling Jen every five minutes for spiritual pep talks, I got all my belongings out of my friend's basement, packed them into nine cardboard boxes, rented a car, drove the boxes to Amtrak, shipped my life across the country, broke my lease, and flew back across the country *again*, landing at home in my parents' house in Maryland.

I blocked said mentor on every medium, as well as every person I met through her. (Fuck it.)

And with Jen's help and my own volition, I decided that if I was ever going to break the spell I was under, I could, would and *had* to protect myself as fiercely as heavenly possible.

Cue: devotion to overcoming, come hell or high water.

I finally surrendered my know-it-all 13-year-old, my too-broke-to-get-help wounded healer, my Bad Girl shame, my endless self-blame. I devoted to getting real professional help.

THE SECRET'S OUT

At this point, I knew all my reserves of self-determination wouldn't be enough to get me where I wanted to go: to the land where my world wasn't controlled by my trauma.

I called on my Facebook community, and without saying too much about why, asked for their recommendations for the best trauma healing modalities. I was pointed to Somatic Experiencing—a modality developed by leading trauma researcher and educator, Peter Levine. I searched his website for a practitioner in the area and what I found was a real life angel. Many angels, actually. I finally began getting the support I needed. I began reading books about trauma, watching videos about trauma, talking to shamans and energy workers about trauma—and suddenly, everything began to click.

I was experiencing *trauma*.

And, there was help for me. Help that would reunite me with an aliveness so luscious I wouldn't be able to believe I'd been living so long without it.

In the next chapter, I'll go into the difference between being bad and being traumatized, as well as the basic inner workings of trauma, scientifically speaking. It's my deep hope, Secret Bad Girl, that you'll be able to begin contextualizing your own story inside the journey of your *physiology*, rather than your psychological stories alone.

We live in a world of incessant self-help messages that, in the case of trauma, can actually serve to cloak the spell even further. Especially at first, expecting yourself to "forgive" or "speak out" or "get better boundaries" or "just love yourself" are all very challenging goals when your whole system's in an altered state of life-or-death hyper-alertness. Sure—you can do your Good Girl enlightened duties with a whole lot of will power. Once. Twice. In moments of highly focused intention. But until you move into your physiology and begin to understand how to regulate *and* transform imprinted traumas, there will be no sustainable transformation, no spontaneous ease, no true embodied freedom.

It took me years of round about journeying to finally find out I was traumatized. Maybe you're in the same boat, and have already been on a circuitous sojourn with your Secret Bad Girl self. Maybe you're under a spell worse than I was. Maybe your cycle's been meaner than mean. Maybe you're thinking it's too late to save yourself from your past.

What I know is it's not too late to break the spell for your future.

And you deserve that, Secret Bad Girl. You deserve to come home to your natural blueprint of health that no experience of violating imprint can ever break or destroy—your aliveness, your light, your unbreakable core of goodness. Life asks a lot of each of us every single day. You deserve to be able to respond from the center of your inherent strength, not the splayed physiology of someone stuck under a spell. You deserve to know that you're not fucked up, bad or wrong for whatever happened to you that's still affecting you. You deserve to feel your resilience, aglow.

This book is a call to bring all of your magic home. The next chapter begins to underline just how.

I EXPLAINED IT MUCH BETTER WHEN HE ASKED, BUT INSIDE IT STILL FELT LIKE THIS

how do you know the
difference between rape and
dominating sex?
*i don't know. i don't know. i
don't know. i don't know*. ***i don't.***

Chapter 3

DESTIGMATIZING THE TRAUMA SPELL

TRAUMA. SOCIETY'S SECRET SPELL.

I remember being in middle school and all the girls in the locker room talking about shaving their coochies. We were 12, our sex was just barely emerging, and we were already on guard with our machetes of contortion. What a thing to think you have to do—a way you think you have to be—to get the love you think you're not worthy of at only 12 years old.

In hindsight, the contrast between bellowing out *Build Me Up Buttercup* and comparing coochies in the middle school gym locker was heartbreaking. But what did I know? I was just a girl who'd watched too much MTV Spring Break and thought that there was nothing abnormal about objectifying my body to gain approval. I was just one of endless Secret Bad Girls, awkwardly giggling as I simultaneously reveled in and avoided my wildness.

That same year, my friend George took me out on his four-wheeler and steered off behind some big marble home sign-post, pulled his pants down, pushed me to my knees and said, "You know what to do. Now do it."

I was 12. He was 12. Who knows "what to do" when they're 12? Why are 12 year olds thinking they should "know what to do down there"? Why hasn't anyone taught them how to "do things" with love, if things are going to be "done" at all? Who planted these seeds? Who's keeping them alive?

Maybe in your story, you avoided biting from the poisonous trauma apple until much later in life. Maybe you were 18 or 22 or 38, and old enough to think you should've known better than "letting happen" whatever happened. Maybe it's crystal clear that you did not "let anything happen," but that someone forced him or herself upon you, plain and terribly simple. Maybe no one pushed you to your knees, penis not yet fully grown, and shoved it in your mouth. (Or maybe someone did. And maybe you were just a kid. If so, I am so incredibly sorry.)

Regardless of your age or consequence, tell me you never watched *Singled Out* or read *Cosmo*, or dieted when you were already skinny, or thought you had to be skinny to be loved—or straight or bigger breasted or funnier or nicer or sluttier.

Tell me you never ate the crops our culture planted, nutritional value: NOT ENOUGH, and maybe then I'll tell you it was your fault for not loving yourself. Maybe then I'll say you should've known better.

Everyone's traumatized to some extent. Everyone's got life-preserving fear pulsing through their bodies because we live in a scary society where it's okay that one in three women get raped, it's okay that we split and frack the earth for gas that's leaking into our clean water, it's okay that we go to war over money, it's okay that we murder out of fear and racism and bigotry and an unwillingness to see all life as sacred.

You're not bad if you couldn't kick the villain off and run. If you chose to partner up with him, pray he'd get you ahead. If you kept promising yourself you wouldn't bite the bait anymore, but somehow still found yourself compulsively biting it anyway.

You're a very normal human, hungry for love and nurture. Hungry to know you matter. Hungry to be fed something as holy and delicious as orgasmic connection. Hungry to feel your body stabilized, and full.

The crop is bad. But it's what you've been fed. You've been eating it. But who could blame you?

THE NATURE OF THE SECRET TRAUMA SPELL

Let me spell this out for you, Secret Bad Girl. Most of the time, when you've experienced trauma, you think that if you go back to the time and place where you first bit the apple, you can have a do-over, and choose differently—choose good.

The problem is the nervous system doesn't work that way. Until you've actually recovered and calmed your reptilian brain—until you've shed the physiological imprints of fear that are layered around your natural blueprint of health (which I'll explain in scientific detail in the next chapter)—the part of you that, unbeknownst to you, has been operating on high alert, stays on high alert. So when you return to that triggering scenario, or when that triggering scenario pops up in your life, your system will respond as if that old violation is still happening.

Which can look like moving into deep dissociation with any hint of violation.

Which can look like over-reactive rage, over something potentially quite small.

Which can look like numbing out with food, alcohol, pot or TV—never allowing yourself to emerge as a bigger or more seen self in the world—out of fear of attracting more triggering experiences.

Which can look like continuously moving across the country whenever life gets squirrely, or being very quick to quit, break up, run, dash, dart from any situation that feels less than comfortable—or *into* any situation that seems exciting.

Which can look like dating people that will reinforce the less-than-ideal imprint you're walking around inside (in either obvious or hidden ways).

Which can look like hiding out from the world, turning all your body's rage inward, and becoming depressed or self-loathing because you don't know to identify your rage as physiological and you have no instructions about how to discharge the secret poison spell.

You're not *bad* if you're experiencing or embodying any of these things. You're one of billions in a wildly surreptitious trauma trance. And I'd say you're ready to learn all about it, so you can break the spell and return to wholeness.

SECRET SEXUALITY

Have you ever hung out with five-year-old girls? I was a nanny to one, and she was the most sensually curious human I'd ever encountered. Because of my background, I was hypersensitive about nurturing her curiosities in a shame-free yet safe and boundaried way. I got to watch her confidence and connection to sensual delight grow and blossom. It was one of the greatest honors of my adult life, thus far.

How many people have that kind of support or safe encouragement as kids? I'd guess that many of us were shamed, yelled at, made fun of, or told we can only revel in our pleasure in private. "Take that to your room, sweetie." Some of us, worse still, perhaps had our innocent nature exploited by someone who we were supposed to trust, like a family member or adult friend. But most definitely, a good portion of our completely innocent five-year-old selves, in one way or another, received the message that our pleasure, our sensuality, our curiosity, our desire, was off-limits, not free, the property of another, inappropriate, corruptible or… *bad.*

As I mentioned at the beginning of the book, my own Secret Bad Girl Club started when I was five, playing "The Game". Taking off all my clothes with girlfriends and running warm body against warm body, maybe kissing or maybe just looking at each other's nipples, giggling all hot-faced and sweaty? Miraculously, I was never caught playing "The Game".

I *was* however caught masturbating in the bathtub when I was 13, legs inverted above me, water streaming hot and strong inside of me. My mom, suspicious that my long "showers" at night were a cover-up for smoking cigarettes, picked the lock, pulled back the curtain, and in shock over what she saw, screamed at me to *Get up! Get out! What are you doing!? Get up!*

Hi, mortification. Hi, feeling fear in my body every time I masturbated for a decade following. Hi, secret trauma. Hi, associating pleasure with being a bad bad bad girl.

HOW DOES GETTING CAUGHT MASTURBAT-ING COUNT AS TRAUMA?

When we hear the word "trauma" most of us go to images of war vets, natural disaster victims, or possibly violent rapes or ongoing molestations. We don't necessarily think our mom walking in on us while masturbating at 13 could have long-term effects on us, other than perhaps some embarrassment or shame.

But trauma's a tricky spell, designed almost flawlessly by the evolution of the human brain to be highly deceptive and difficult to detect. It also happens on a spectrum. For example, someone who's experienced a single-instance rape as an adult is going to have a different resolution process than someone who's experienced incest as a child or someone who's experiencing the trauma of compounded generational or systemic violence. All of this will vary from someone who's done two deployments to combat zones, and outlived many of his or her friends.

Additionally, we can experience trauma in many

ways. As intense instances of violence and violation (rape, assault, or molestation, for example). As cultural or societal undertones that sometimes emerge with overt offenses, and other times loom as inherent threats (expressions of racism or sexism, for example). As the aftermath of never recovering or getting breathing room from those intense violations or violences, which can often result in things like sleep-walking through our sexual choices, partaking in addictive avoidance behaviors, or choosing re-traumatizing situations as subconscious attempts to find healing or closure.

We can experience trauma tangentially or via witnessing an experience that violates our sense of safety in the world. Watching war or shootings on the news can be traumatizing, for example. Hearing your daughter's story of being raped, and feeling as though you should've been able to protect her, can be traumatizing. Witnessing a violent car accident—even if you didn't actually crash—can have traumatizing effects.

All of these examples are things that can activate the reptilian brain that's responsible for ensuring survival, and cloak our natural blueprints of health with imprints of stress and fear.

Luckily, no stress is too big to regulate, and our bodies have incredible inherent treatment plans that know how to restore us to health and aliveness if we give them the space and attention to bring forth their brilliance. Even as stress is ongoing, we can bring resolution to cycles of trauma with a good understanding about how trauma works, as well as tried and true resolution practices, both of which I'll explain in the next two chapters.

NONSENSE

dissociative
is a five syllable word.
very convenient,
thought the poet with more rapes
than fingers, or reasons why.

Chapter 4

THE SCIENCE OF TRAUMA

THE SECRET BAD GIRL BRAIN

We've covered a lot already in this book. I've shared with you my personal story of traumatic imprinting, a bit about my life under the trauma spell, how I discovered that I was suffering from trauma, and the difference between living with trauma and being "bad". Part two of the book is going to talk all about trauma resolution—physiological, psychological and spiritual resolution. Before we go any further though, it's time to learn about the secret brain science of trauma in eight simple concepts. Because when you can bring educated awareness to the unconscious workings of your nervous system and brain, you can become an empowered facilitator of breaking your trauma spell.

But first, the big question: What exactly IS trauma?

My working definition of trauma is really simple.

Trauma is an embodied violation hangover. In other words, trauma is the residual energy that's stuck in one's body long after a violation, shock, or dangerous experience has occurred. The only difference between a violation hangover and a substance hangover, is a violation hangover can last much, much longer; weeks, months, years, decades—even intergenerational periods of time.

Why is this? Why does the energy of violation stay stuck in the human body, rather than leave when the violation is over? It has to do with the way we're wired, from brain to body. These 8 concepts will help paint the picture of what's going on below our cognitive awareness that creates an opportunity for the energy of violation to linger in our bodies long after violation has ended.

8 CONCEPTS FOR UNDERSTANDING THE BRAIN SCIENCE OF TRAUMA

1.   THE BODY HAS NATURAL RESPONSES TO THREAT.

Every human has an Autonomic Nervous System (ANS). The ANS controls your organ functions, sleep, digestion, sweat… anything that happens without your cognitive awareness. It also controls your super-duper fast response to danger (think: capacity to run faster, hit harder, or stand exceptionally still—depending on which one would better serve to save your life) without ever giving you the cognitive chance to think about it.

2.   THESE AUTOMATIC DANGER-RESPONSES ARE YOUR LIFE-SAVING INSTINCTS.

They're also known as Fight, Flight or Freeze. When your body is facing a threat to its survival, it either fights the threat (attacks it), flights from the threat (gets far away as fast as possible), or freezes (dissociates or plays dead). All three of these automatic responses are designed to protect from pain and ensure survival.

3. THE BODY CHOOSES SURVIVAL OVER HIGHER-LEVEL "REASON."

Our Fight, Flight or Freeze responses (and entire ANS) are controlled by our reptilian brain. When the reptilian brain gets hyperactivated, the neocortex and limbic brains, which control our higher-level thinking (such as relational intelligence or verbal skills) have *less cognitive capacity*. Therefore, your ability to "make good choices" or "reason your way out" of something becomes deeply impaired once your ANS gets triggered. *However*, with a triggered ANS, your body activates intense adrenaline that generally ensures your *survival*.

4. NEXT, THE BODY EITHER USES, STORES OR DISCHARGES ITS FIGHT, FLIGHT OR FREEZE ENERGY.

After a triggering event takes place, the body and brain can return to a state of health if the energy from the activation is either fully embodied (the fight or flight saves you from experiencing pain) or fully discharged (the freeze state of dissociation gets shaken out of the body after it's no longer needed). This is the ideal scenario. On the other hand, if one does not fully embody fight or flight, or does not fully release freeze—the activation from the violation can remained stored in the body.

5.   OFTEN, HIGHER LEVEL THINKING COMES BACK ONLINE, HALTING THE FREEZE DISCHARGE PROCESS.

Discharging an activation is part of the reptilian brain's natural response. However, once a triggering event has ended, the neocortex and limbic brains (home of that high-level reasoning) usually come back online, stopping the completion of the reptilian brain's physiological discharge, and instead moving into emotional and cognitive processing.

6.   WHEN IDEAL DISCHARGE DOESN'T HAPPEN, ACTIVATED ENERGIES WREAK HAVOC ON YOUR SYSTEM.

While your higher-level brain is trying to make sense of the experience you've just had, your physiology is still either coursing with Fight or Flight energy, or stuck in the stupor of Freeze energy. When those energies remain active in you, they turn into an imprint of trauma that interferes with the embodiment of your natural blueprint of health. (Remember—Fight, Flight or Freeze are natural and healthy responses when a triggering event is *happening*, but after the event is over, those energies generally become destructive.)

7.   WHEN YOUR NATURAL RESPONSE SYSTEM NEVER FINISHES ITS DISCHARGE PROCESS, YOU'RE LEFT WITH TRAUMA.

Peter Levine, world-renowned trauma researcher

and specialist would say that *this* is when "trauma" becomes active. *After* the activating event has occurred, when your system is still being influenced by an "incomplete physiological response suspended in fear", you then "qualify" as living with trauma. In many cases, this trauma will remain in your body until you work to move it out.

8.   IT'S NEVER TOO LATE TO FINISH THE PROCESS.

Luckily, when we are made aware of the looping pattern of our physiology and autonomic nervous system, we can begin the process of discharging the residual activation energy, and return to our natural blueprints of health and aliveness. We can break the trauma spell.

Before moving on, I'd like to explain a bit more about the body's regulation and the its movement into fight, flight and freeze, as well as the possible responses for dealing with experiences of a traumatic activation.

The following are teachings I learned from Brigit Viksnins, an incredible healer I've both worked with and studied under in her powerful trauma resolution training program called Alchemical Alignment.

FIGHT, FLIGHT AND FREEZE

Every human body has this cool thing called "**neuroception.**" Neuroception is the subconscious system in the body for detecting threat and danger. It explains why a baby coos at her own caregiver, but cries at strangers.

When your neuroception (or embodied perception of threat) goes up, it's as if your nervous system unconsciously moves up a metaphorical ladder—from the most grounded level of *regulation* at the bottom rung, then up to *hypersocialization* at the next rung, then up another rung to *fight* or *flight*, and then finally, on the top rung, the nervous system suspends itself in *freeze*.

Regulation is the place where we'd ideally like to hang out as human beings. At the bottom of the metaphorical ladder, it's grounded and stable and safe. It's where the magic of health and aliveness lives. When you've got a regulated nervous system, you can do things like digest your foods, sleep, orgasm, multitask, express yourself, relate comfortably with others, feel passion and drive and creativity and bounce back from difficult experiences. You have clearly defined boundaries, and it feels like second nature to uphold them.

Hypersocialization is the first rung up the metaphorical ladder of nervous system hyperactivation. It's a slightly heightened state of hyperawareness about others, in which taking care of their needs, checking in on their feelings and managing their stress become mechanisms for attempting to control your own sense of safety. The subconscious line of thought is something like, "If I keep others at bay, I will be safe."

The **fight** and **flight** responses, another rung up the ladder, both happen when the nervous system gets even more hyperactivated by perceived threat. In these states, your body may begin feeling hot, internal and external pacing may speed up, and anxiety, stress, anger or rage may awaken more and more. Things tend to feel out of control in the fight or flight response, and decisions are made quite quickly and subconsciously. With the fight response, the activated energy would move *toward* the threat in an attempt to protect you, while with the flight response, the activated energy would move *away* from the threat in an attempt to protect you.

When the hyperactivity of fight and flight become too overwhelming and your nervous system senses with greatest fear that it may not survive, the **freeze** response kicks in, and slows everything down to a *hypo*activation of possible dissociation and numbing out or depression and lethargy. A literally cold and stiff body can come online at this point. At the top of the metaphorical ladder, your cognition floats "up in the clouds" as a way to keep your body from feeling any pain that may be happening down on earth.

People with developmental trauma can sometimes have "worm holes" of self-protection available for scurrying into as soon as they sense threat. In other words, habitual responses lodged deep in the nervous system, like "going into a dark hole of depression" or "laying in bed for a whole day" can be almost instantly skipped to if someone with extreme developmental trauma senses threat or is under extreme stress.

Although these concepts may sound quite dismal, it's not all doom and gloom. Not at all. Trauma has the capacity to expel, transform and complete. In fact, not only can it complete, but it can actually go extinct. Yes, extinct! More on that below.

STABILIZATION AND COMPLETION

While there's a metaphorical ladder the nervous system climbs up when the body perceives danger or threat, there's also a slide the nervous system can go down when it's ready to resolve the activated energy.

This "slide" can go in one direction, or another. In the first direction, the slide is more like a temporary fix to the activated nervous system, and it's called "**stabilization**". Stabilization is when you soothe or distract yourself from the activation through any number of mechanisms—meditation, exercise, substances, television, calling on a close confidant, playing with the dog. Stabilization brings you back down from your autonomic nervous system's activation spike, avoiding looping in a hijacked trauma spell.

Down the other side of the slide is "**completion**". With completion, by focusing on your natural blueprint of health (usually with the assistance of a professional guide) your autonomic nervous system can actually expel traumatic imprints from your body in waves. This process, taken a few steps farther, can actually lead to "**extinction**"—where the physiological memory of the triggering experience is completely gone, and your body returns to its fullest state of health and aliveness, with no threat of being triggered by something old in the future.

ANIMALS HOLD THE SECRET SPELL BREAKER

Conveniently, humans and animals share the reptilian brain—the part of the brain that's instinctually activated in response to overwhelming threat. And yet, animals rarely experience trauma after threat—even threat that nearly kills them—while humans very often do. Why is that?

In reading Peter Levine's work, I've learned that from

an evolutionary perspective, animals have a clear delineation between predator and prey, and thus, those that know their clear role as prey (an impala in the wild, for instance), have become intimate and well-versed in their survival resources. They know what to do in the face of a sharp-toothed fast-as-lightning cheetah—and they do it. There's no second-guessing because *there's no other choice.*

When chased: run or die. When caught: dissociate or suffer. When the cheetah's dragged the impala home thinking it's dead in its dissociative state, then leaves it by a rock and trots off for a sip of water from the stream before coming back to feast, the impala either gets up and runs—fast—or gets eaten. And finally, when the impala has saved its own life with its Autonomic Nervous System response and gotten itself to a place of safety, it either shakes out the residual flight and freeze energies that are left over from the attack, or suffers as a weakened entity and becomes easy prey in the future. Live or die. Bounce back or become easy prey. Two choices only.

Humans, on the other hand, have a genetic memory of being both predator *and* prey. Before the development of tools that could be used for hunting or self-defense, humans were much more vulnerable as prey. Think: no sharp teeth, not that fast, and highly susceptible to attack. So today, the genetic memory of being easy prey has sustained in our brains and nervous systems, resulting in a *deep uncertainty that we can save our own lives.* This explains the waffling back and forth between the reptilian brain and the neo-cortex/limbic brain.

Additionally, we've now developed our predator capacities a thousand fold—however, not through our bodies, but through our minds. And because our higher-level minds are so developed, we tend to override our *physiological* wisdom, making us particularly susceptible to trauma. (Yes, it's quite the double bind).

When the brain is stuck inside a trauma spell—meaning the reptilian part is hyperactivated, and the higher-level parts are less accessible—it feels almost like having a slight brain injury to your innate brilliance. Functioning goes down and one has to try a lot harder to access the naturally intelligent mind.

This might be totally depressing to read, but it's actually one of my favorite things to tell clients or people I talk to who are suffering inside the trauma spell, because it comes with some good news. I like to use this metaphor: when the brain's functioning with activated trauma, it's like swimming with two bathing suits on—training for a big race. When you take off the extra bathing suit—when you resolve your trauma—you're going to be able to move further than ever before with more grace and ease than you ever could've imagined.

So again, if you're feeling like something is wrong with you—like perhaps you're stupid, bad, or forever flawed, I'd like to suggest the possibility that it's not your fault, but rather, your brain has been hijacked by trauma. And—subsequently—recovery happens. Your brain regressions *can reverse*, leaving you with the more refined mind you always hoped was inside.

I also tend to think that people who experience intense bouts under the trauma spell, and then lift themselves out of it, have more intimate access to a number of incredible things that others may never experience: feelings of immense emotional and physical resilience, deep empathy for profound suffering, heightened capacity for intensity, great power, strength, determination and will to thrive, and a particularly alive zest for pleasure.

While we need to rely on our animal instincts to help us fully resolve our traumas, in the end, after we shed the residual fear imprints from our systems, we get access to the best of both worlds: the embodied vitality of the animal world, and the enhanced emotionality and intellect of the human world.

YOUR INNER-ANIMAL: THE LIFE-SAVER

Before moving onto the six keys for trauma resolution, I want to mention one more time just how intelligent your Autonomic Nervous System is, to clear any stigma you may be feeling or experiencing. For example, have you ever secretly thought you were stupid for dissociating? For not kicking the person off?

The "freeze" or immobility response of the ANS is tricky for the human mind to make sense of, accept, and work with. Often, we label dissociation as a shameful, weak or cowardly response to threat—something that signals we weren't strong enough to break out of a shady or scary situation.

However, let me say this loud and clear: you are not weak, cowardly or defective for dissociating. Entering into a dissociative "immobility response" is your biological, instinctual, *unconscious* response to threat or violation. And it can actually be the very thing that saves your life. In freezing, the human body enters an altered state in which little to no pain is experienced.

Next, have you ever thought you were crazy, out of control, mentally ill or a straight-up bitch for continually going off on people? People who may or may not be doing something "worth" going off about? Hello, fight response! Again, if this is consistently happening, it's likely that your nervous system is being triggered by an old imprint of violation, sensing the potential for violation in someone else's actions, and doing the smartest thing it knows in order to try to save your life: fight like a mother fucker. (I'm not "excusing" or condoning this behavior because I do believe everyone must take personal responsibility for their actions, but I am attempting to de-stigmatize it by saying that it's quite possible you're still operating within a hijacked nervous system that's far more likely to unconsciously respond with "fight" when triggered or threatened.)

Last, have you ever thought you were flaky, wildly irresponsible, fickle, or far too impulsive for up and leaving any job, relationship, friendship or family that felt potentially violating or unsafe? For simply not calling the dude back? This would be your flight response, picking up on a signal of danger, and doing the best thing it knows in order to save your life: leave.

While each of these responses comes with stigmatized reputations that are hard to shed emotionally, I'd like to take a moment to simply appreciate our human survival instincts. The way we naturally protect ourselves from pain by shutting down or zoning out. The way we fight that which may violate our beauty or our sacredness. The way we flee what feels like unhealthy situations.

Ultimately, we humans are wise and brilliant beings. It's just that sometimes our most natural intelligence gets stuck looping in the wrong place, at the wrong time. Of course, the more we know, the more empowered we become to take responsibility for the ways that our past may still be showing up and screwing with our present. Which is why it's my great pleasure to share with you the six key ingredients for resolving trauma (stories included!), so that your can more easily reclaim your inherent brilliance, and bring it back online, at the right places and the right times.

TIME AND TRAUMA

One question I'm consistently asked is, "How long will it take for me to resolve my trauma?"

Here's my answer: there is no magic "recovery estimation time" for trauma resolution. Trauma "resolution" isn't even always what happens. Sometimes imprints stay with us forever. Not because we're broken or unfixable or not trying or screwed by the fates. But because sometimes, part of what it means to be human is to learn to make space for the things we can't control, the scars that never leave, the pain that (perhaps in some fucked up way) was meant to (or simply did) break us.

There's a defiant kind of love that can birth in the woman who refuses to hate her pain. The woman who chooses to slash around in it, dance with it, claim it as part of her magic, wallow in it whenever she feels like it—do these things *in choice*, consciously, on purpose. *My trauma. My pain. My responsibility. My right to make art or mess or sinful ecstatic expression out of it.*

Each person's journey is unique and deeply personal. Claiming your pain can be a big part of your resolution.

I will say this much, though: while trauma resolution can happen mystically, mythically, creatively and somatically, it does not happen effortlessly. It also usually costs something. Something financial. Something personal. Something energetic. Definitely something of courage and conviction.

Depending on how deep and extensive your trauma runs—at what age you experienced it, how recurring it was, what your response was, what kind of support you received during the time—resolution could take anywhere from months to years.

Healing (with all things) often also depends on how much you fear the consequences, or what it would cost you, to experience that healing. If you know your healing would bank on leaving a somewhat abusive relationship, but the cost of that would be really scary to you, change will be slower. If you're afraid of putting the dollars in to get the help you know you need the most, your stalling will stall your healing.

None of theses statements come with any judgment. Sometimes we want to move slow. Sometimes, as you'll learn in the next chapter, slow equals safety… and aggregating safety is such a huge part of how we heal.

I personally invested 3 to 4 years and tens of thousands of dollars of money I didn't have because even though I was scared of debt, I was more scared of spiraling forever. (It was worth it.) I also moved home to my parents house because even though I wanted to finish out my twenties surrounded by peers, having a good time, and even though I was afraid that living with my parents would mean never meeting a new romantic partner and being totally unhappy, it was the stability I needed to feel like I could invest in my healing. (Again, worth it. And, for the record, I met an incredible love.)

All of this said, I do believe my resolution could've happened a lot faster and cheaper had I known about trauma resolution therapies sooner. Why? Because trauma resolution (with a good practitioner) is exceptionally efficient.

For example, the body stores our memories energetically. When we experience a violation of a certain theme (say: a violation where we lose our voice), and then that imprint attracts recurring violations of the same theme, we begin to form a sort of embodied energetic pattern of "when x happens, I lose my voice." In trauma resolution, it's possible to spend one or two sessions recovering your voice (through somatic, interpersonal techniques, not just psychological ones), and your body can gain the capacity to *both* shift the pattern of "when x happens, I lose my voice," *and* shed from your embodied *memory* many instances of voice-loss. In other words, you can heal many memories—both in the body, and in the psyche—in one fell swoop.

Again—trauma resolution, in my experience, is extremely efficient.

Now, it's with my great pleasure that I give a bit more detail about the six key ingredients for breaking the trauma spell.

Part 2

SPIRALING GRACE

i am following the portal
through a dark dripping cave
shards, glittering deep

crawling through a cold hole—
my knees collecting sparkling battle scars of faith,
my elbows earning cataclysmic strength—
nothing—nothing can stay the same

i am giving up on blame,
crouching like a black panther
eyes aglow, knowing
i am entering
the other side
of my soul

The first step in breaking the trauma spell is knowing the spell was cast. The second is learning how to break it. After reading about my life under the trauma spell, as well as the science and inner-workings of how trauma operates, hopefully you have a better understanding about whether or not you've been living under a trauma spell. If you have been, the good news is I've got six key ingredients you can use to break it and reclaim your natural aliveness and joy.

THE 6 KEY INGREDIENTS FOR BREAKING THE TRAUMA SPELL

1) Move slowly.
2) Realign the body to its natural blueprint of health and release stale imprints.
3) Repattern your mind and spirit for new ways of thriving.
4) Experiment with new edges AND embrace new boundaries.
5) Forgive. (Yourself and others.)
6) Revel in your aliveness.

Each of these key ingredients has its own chapter in part two of the book, but first, a note about order.

While I do recommend this order when possible, in reality, healing trauma is more like making a stew than baking a cake. And thank god, because I've notoriously failed at all things baking.

Also, just in case you're wondering, I did all of these things out of order. Doubled back on some (a few times!) and am still practicing every single one of them in my daily life, today. You'll probably zigzag through and double back, too. And who cares.

Maybe order is meant to be divine more than locked into arbitrary steps disguised as Important Rules for Recovery. Maybe the only rule that matters is you have to want to recover from the illusion that your inherent self is bad. And maybe even that rule isn't completely true.

Maybe no matter what, life sends each of us on a wild goose chase of change, tossing us strangely shaped puzzle pieces of excruciating life events that we can't imagine belonging to us, let alone creating something potentially beautiful.

For me, that happened over and over again, until one day I found myself truly changed at the end of a gruesome and glorious 15-year shit show, feeling awe-struck and baffled that it all added up to beautiful, vibrant, confident, safe... me. My nervous system recovered. My blueprint came back online. I really did resolve past trauma. (Those stories still to come!) Sure, I'm still human. I still get triggered sometimes. But I am significantly more empowered and at ease than ever before in my life.

These days, the whole long saga is starting to look more like destiny than disaster—even when some of the stories feel particularly hard to share, even when my life's still a work in progress. Like it or not, my wild goose chase of zigzagging change? It all truly mattered.

And I believe yours will, too.

LOVABLE

is resting cheating?
no. resting is not cheating.
it is resting.

is eating cheating?
is drinking cheating?
is not going to yoga cheating?

no. it is eating.
it is drinking.
it is not going to yoga.

and it is really,
truly,
honestly
OKAY.

because there's nothing
i have to do
to prove that
i'm lovable.

let me repeat that for myself...
lovingly...
there is nothing
i have to do...
softens eyes, lowers shoulders
smiles like looking at a child
to prove that
i'm lovable.

i just am.
just as is.

tired poems,
massive doubts,
self-hating shouts and all.

still lovable.

Chapter 5

THE SPEED OF RESOLUTION

KEY 1: MOVE SLOWLY.

"Can you just be where you are for a little while, without trying to get somewhere else, so fast?" This is what my dear friend Karen asked me, days after I got my surgery in Maryland, when I was practically sprinting back to Portland. If only I'd listened to Karen!

Instead, with my nervous system spiked from the triggering pain of having surgery on my vulva, I made a move under the trauma spell and sped *back* to Portland before I'd had time to recover.

Ripe for a trigger to set me into a looping frenzy, I found one. It was at this point when I had that violating evening with my mentor-boss, spiraled deeper than ever before, and ended up moving *back* across the country for the fourth time in three months.

Of course, at the time, I thought all of this was because I was "crazy", "flighty", "insane" and "irresponsible". Later learning about and understanding how trauma works truly saved my self-perception.

All this to say, when I talk about "moving slowly" as the first key to trauma resolution, I do, indeed mean moving slowly in your external life. Choosing to sleep on decisions. Choosing to allow yourself more time in your schedule for things like meditation, yoga, cooking healthy meals, and time in nature or with rejuvenating friends. Perhaps not moving across the country four times in three months. (*Wink.*)

There's nothing a looping nervous system loves more than speed. It keeps it reaming, and then eventually sets it streaming down deep into freeze—which is the body's greatest way to feel safe. And yes—your nervous system wants to keep you safe! So when it perceives threat, it can actually be very difficult convincing it to slow down.

And yet, your soul and your natural blueprint of health know that you're not meant to be living so fast and furious or so quietly ashamed. These truest parts of you love slow, love stable—yes, they love adventure, too, but on healthy terms, not when spurred from a place of fear. When you go slow, when you surrender to the flow of stillness, you invite the miracle of your blueprint back online.

Here's a little story of how I found a key part of mine.

THE MEDITATING RABBIT

I was lying on a dusty rug in a Bedouin tent at Burning Man, an annual festival of spiritual exploration and radical self-expression in the middle of the Nevada desert. A shaman, banging on his drum, was inducing a trance-like state for myself and a circle of other spiritually eager Burners who'd shown up to a "Discovering Your Spirit Animal" workshop.

Bada boom, bada boom, bada boom.

The rhythm moved me deeper in. Down the slithering slide of my mind, through my oscillating lungs, far behind my tongue, perhaps… perhaps to where my spirit animal was waiting.

"An animal is here to greet you," this tiny shaman announced with the grandeur of God inside him.

I wasn't *really* expecting it, but suddenly, there he was. An upright, all white, mischievous meditating RABBIT.

My mind came back online for a moment of objection. I knew a thing or two about animal totems, and what I knew of rabbit, I did not like. In my school of thought, rabbit was representative of fear—calling in all your worst demons. Sure, perhaps to alchemize them, but still—*no thanks!*

Bada boom, bada boom, bada boom.

The thumping shamanic drumming pulled me back in.

"Observe your animal. Do not fight what you see," said the tiny godly shaman. "Watch its messaging. It has things to tell you, show you, teach you."

I watched as my meditative rabbit sat, unafraid of any madness—mischievous and ecstatic and *still*. His ears pointed straight up like cypress trees. His hands rested in lotus on his cross-legged knees. His eyes were slit wide—wider than the tent, wider than the desert, wider than the sky. He was wise, alert, aware, and *still*. Yet, in his stillness, it almost seemed as if the speed of light could move right through him. And then, it did. A flash of everything hot and holy coursed through me, and my whole body, mind and perception became bright white goodness.

Sometimes, when we're moving extra slow—slower than slow—when we allow ourselves to become still, we become portals for the energy of everything stale to be seen and wiped clean. My meditating rabbit is still with me today. In fact, before every session I have with clients, I call him into my body, awaken his energy, employ him to help me create a container for old energy to clear at the speed of light and be replaced by the holy white truth at the core of every human.

THE MAGIC WHALE

I'm not the only one who utilizes animal energies to tap into epic states of stillness and alchemy. During one of my first sessions with healer Brigit, she led me through a small visualization of imagining myself as a whale. Specifically, a gigantic ancient whale at the very bottom of the ocean, moving exceptionally fast, yet feeling exceptionally still. This transcendental visualization made it feel as though I could bend space and time—manipulate the energies moving through me—directing anything especially hot or especially cold out of my body, and returning myself to my regulated and aligned natural blueprint of health.

It may sound a bit kooky—but this capacity to bring stillness into one's body is a key ingredient for resolving trauma. It's a power—a *super* power—to move slow and steady, intentional but ready to resolve. When we allow ourselves to move from this altered state of presence, we can watch the waves of information and activation that may arise when we're triggered by past traumas. As these waves arise, the greater our capacity to observe, the greater our capacity to allow the waves to naturally move their way out. This is when real life magic happens.

There's a skill in trauma resolution called **pendulation** that very much relies on your capacity to slow and still. With pendulation, you focus all your attention on a resource—either a part of your body that feels stable, balanced, grounded or neutral, a place in nature that calms your spirit, a person who brings you joy, or a talisman of sorts that brings you power or peace. By focusing on a resource that you can access in the moment, you bring a feeling of safety and stability to your nervous system. With more safety and stability, your nervous system unclenches from the stronghold of traumatic fear, and that activated energy has the opportunity to move up and out of your system.

So often, we rush to focus on the "problems" we're experiencing. And it's true, even with trauma, that what we focus on has greater likelihood of growth. Instead of focusing on the "negative", with pendulation, you slowly and intentionally bring all of your attention to your identified *resource*. Then, you take note of how you know it's a resource, according to your body's cues. For example, perhaps it calms your breath, relaxes your muscles, stills your mind, or makes you smile.

After identifying physiological cues that tell you you indeed have a resource available in the moment, you can slowly shift your attention to a less comfortable part of your body, or the part of you that's activated or looping, while keeping soft awareness on your resource. Moving back and forth between the activated part of you and your identified resource, your energetic and physical body will often begin feeling safe and grounded enough to release old traumatic imprints.

With the care of a specialized professional who understands how to ground the cycles of expansion and contraction that happen as trauma releases—pendulation can be an especially safe and magical way of slowly and naturally dancing towards the completion of a traumatic memory.

So—whatever part of the process you end up diving into first, Secret Bad Girl, remember these stories of the Meditating Rabbit and the Magic Whale. Remember that every time you find a way to slow or still your outer or inner world, you empower your capacity to manage and steer physiological intensity. You become the director of your trauma rather than the victim of it.

One more thing that backs up this invitation. The mind moves approximately eight times faster than the body. Which means, again, any time you still your mind, you're giving your body the chance to employ its inherent healing capacities, without having to respond to the mind's directions. You allow yourself to drop back down into the brilliance of the reptilian brain, where that unfinished game of your natural response to danger can shake, expel and filter what's no longer meant to be with you.

BONUS. Because I know this kind of stilling and slowing can be especially difficult to cultivate on your own, I've created a short meditation to help get you in the zone. Head right over to my book website to try it: www.secretbadgirlfreebies.com

BUT SITTING STILL FEELS LIKE HELL, AND I KIND OF HATE YOU FOR SUGGESTING IT

Smart Secret Bad Girl, I fricking love you for thinking that.

There are one hundred reasons why someone with a history of trauma might really, *really* hate meditation or sitting still. I'll talk here about the two most obvious scientific reasons, and how with trauma resolution, your version of "stillness" can look a whole lot different than perhaps anyone's ever suggested.

First: if your body has a history of being forced to do things against your will, most often, that body has a strong relationship with the "freeze" response, in which the core clenches and constricts, and the limbs and extremities cool or numb. In freeze mode, the body may give you an *illusion* of stillness, but in actuality, what's experienced is more like *lifelessness*. So naturally, if you have an embodied history of perceiving stillness as lifelessness, why would any part of you want to move toward it?

Next: the process of waking up from a long-held "freeze" state generally includes moving into and through the agitation states of "fight" and "flight". When a body is ready to release traumatic imprints, it actually *requires* some sort of movement. That movement can come in the form of *internal* energetic movement (watching waves of heat or colors or images leave your body, for example), or *integrated* energetic movement, in which energy movement and body movement happen at the same time. (Asserting your capacity to push, run or shout are extreme examples of integrated energetic movement. Martial arts, yoga, dance, or running are also examples of integrated energetic movement that moves energy in more subtle, stabilizing ways, making space for the trauma to release over the aggregate.)

When it comes to observing *internal* energetic releases, physical stillness is quite helpful. However, not all people or bodies will want to release trauma in a solely internal kind of way. Many may, in fact, prefer releasing trauma by moving the energy and body *simultaneously*. Additionally, these preferences generally shift and oscillate. After one method has been used with great success, you may find yourself ready or interested in accessing the release potential that the other method could grant you.

What does this mean if you notoriously dislike meditation or sitting still? Your body, at this point in time, may be better suited for *external* energetic releases. Find a yoga, dance or martial arts class that you love. Go on hikes whenever you can. Let your body feel the strength and resilience of legs pounding the pavement on regular runs. Anything that feels grounding, stabilizing, enlivening and empowering. Anything that puts you *in the zone*. Because if you can get in the zone—that meditative state of letting your body find its rhythm, its bearings, its home inside of itself—this is when embodied insights arise, cathartic cries come out of nowhere, memories revisit and release, and your body begins to reclaim its own sovereign state of strength and power.

I write more about whole-body reclamation in the next chapter. But first, check out the questions and practice ideas below about identifying your current "life speed" and reclaiming the rhythms and practices that bring you back to stable.

KEY 1 QUESTIONS AND PRACTICES:

What's your current "life speed"?
If you were to look at your life through the lens of stability, hypersocialization, fight, flight, and freeze, how would you categorize where you are right now? Are you exhibiting the steady aliveness and resilience of stability? The mild anxiety and people-pleasing of hypersocialization? The more quickened speed and panic of fight or flight? The lethargy, depression, or depletion of freeze? Write it out on a piece of paper. Let it live in simple, true words.

Based on your assessment of your current "life speed", do you sense your body needs a "pick-me-up" practice, a "shake it out" practice, a "ground me down" practice, or some combination of all three?
What's your intuitive hunch about what your body needs most? It won't necessarily be the opposite of your current speed. For example, sometimes people with a lot of fight or flight energy, benefit greatly from regular runs. Write it down. Anywhere. Everywhere. Then make a plan in the next day or two to give your body what it wants.

Take a few deep breaths into your belly. Is there an animal that comes to mind, that wants to help you return to regulated rhythms right now?
If so, what traits does that animal embody? (Remember—both movement and stillness may emerge. Both are okay!) Where in your body would this animal like to live? Can you imagine letting it in there? What would it have you do right now? Can you allow yourself to do

it—either in your mind, with tiny micro movements, or full-fledged?

Is there a meditative practice that you've gotten out of touch with?
If so, what is it? Choose 1 to 3 days in the next 7 days that you can re-commit to playing with it... even if it's only for 5 minutes a day. Put it on your calendar. Ask a friend to play with you.

ROUGHED UP

i don't know you and you don't know me
but the sun's out today and everything looks blonde n'
free

gutters glitter with broken sporks n' corner-store bags
trees are barren, web-shadows are cast

i'm dancing my recovery
at last, at last, at last

trembles snake through me
i crack, i crack, i crack

the others dance past me
i'm thankful for that

the long night teaches a thousand ways to say *no*
it's hard to grow so strong
and unladylike

Chapter 6

RELEASE AND RETURN

KEY 2: REALIGN THE BODY TO ITS NATURAL BLUEPRINT OF HEALTH AND RELEASE STALE IMPRINTS.

At the beginning of my trauma recovery, Secret Bad Girl, I DIYed a majority of my healing. I did a lot of self-assessment about what my body was craving, and found myself crazy-devoted to Bikram yoga, ecstatic dance and acupuncture. I took long walks in the woods and sat by the river in Portland. I wrote angry poems. I listened to Caroline Myss on tape (Energy Anatomy via Sounds True is the best). I simply did what felt like health or catharsis.

Later, when my system got too activated to rely on DIY healing alone, I turned to more tried and true trauma-specific help.

I'm telling you all the stories here, because every bit

of it mattered. And in case you don't have the cash to get professional help right now, hopefully, in this chapter, you'll see just how much the body can do on its own.

Speaking of Caroline Myss—she's known for popularizing the concept that your *biography* is your *biology*. In other words, your history creates and lives in your body. But your body can also *shed* its history, because ultimately, you are more than the experiences that have happened to you. You are, and always will be, your original blueprint of health. These stories tell the tale of shaking off my history and re-connecting with the original me.

DANCING IN HELL BEFORE BREAKING THE SPELL

When I got back from the bike trip, in that eight months time of mostly lying around depressed before Brian and I split, I did have *one thing* I got... obsessed with. Dancing.

It was weird. And sweet. And amazing.

Every day, in the kitchen, wearing turquoise arm and leg warmers and one of Jen's green goddess dresses, I'd turn on Alela Diane's To Be Still album (a slow folksy nostalgic kind of album), and let my soul unfold in movement.

I'd sweat. I'd cry. I'd dramatize my emotions just to let them have their full vibrato. I'd light some sage and dance to another song.

I got so obsessed with these winter kitchen dances that I truly began to believe they could, in fact, save the world.

Enter: the Delicious Body Dance-a-Thon.

I decided I'd make videos of my cathartic dancing twice a week for a month or two, and invite my blogger friends to join me. (*Why not!*) A few brave souls joined in, and week after week, we'd watch each other's bodies speak across the pixels. It was magical—to experience myself coming back to life, to watch my friends having their own awakenings, to wake up, together. It was like DIY ecstatic dance for people in places where dance communities didn't exist. Total bliss.

Then, when I moved to Portland, week after week for two whole years, every Wednesday and Sunday, I'd show up to a ballroom of two hundred dancing people and, again, play with the ways that my body wanted to come all the way awake.

Dancing with others proved to be more difficult than dancing in the kitchen on camera. It brought in the relational components of navigating boundaries, fearing outside violation, and questions like, *How sexy can I be, and still feel safe? How much can I express, without attracting distress? How much of my power is permissible here, without getting me into trouble?*

It took six months before terror didn't pulse through my body, or exhaustion didn't wipe me out, every time I danced. But eventually, I was roaring on the floor, twirling with partners, asserting my yeses and noes, owning my beautiful whole goddess of a body and soul.

With each dance, I became more connected to my center. With each rattle, I shed imprints of shame and trauma. With each move of truth, I swayed closer to my natural blueprint of health.

Two years spent well.

THE BODY STORES THE SECRET. THE BODY KNOWS HOW TO FREE IT.

During one of my long bouts of celibacy, exhausted by and terrified of sex, I took up Bikram yoga as my new religion. (Let's not leave out that Bikram Choudhury, creator of Bikram yoga, has been accused on multiple counts of rape! Go figure.) I'd go to 30 days of Bikram in a row, take a few days off, then do another 30 just for fun. By normal standards, this is absolute insanity.

If you've never heard of Bikram, it's a 90-minute yoga class at 105 degrees that repeats the same 26 postures in the same order each time—and the postures are not easy breezy. The teachers memorize a script that's given in nearly the same way each class. "Make your body flat like a Japanese ham sandwich." "Grip the bottom of your feet with Bengal tiger strength." Some teachers bark, some sing. Either way, it's intense.

But for some reason Bikram activated a highly meditative state for me. (Cue: *integrated* energetic movement.) I became so accustomed to the rhythm of this 90-minute moving meditation that my practices felt like stillness, and my awareness of my internal landscape became hyper-awake and sensitive.

One day, after a particularly hot Bikram class, I ran to the bathroom and vomited, then collapsed on the dressing room floor convulsing in tears. After the fireworks of barf and wailing subsided, an eerie calm swooped over me, my eyes shut, and I received image after image of two women in my family line being raped, like a visual download of a movie.

A week later, I asked one of these women about the

images I saw of her. Shocked, she confirmed their accuracy.

This experience felt like ever more proof that trauma lives in the body and can be transferred down our lineage through DNA. That our bodies store the secret, and our bodies know how to free it. That we must learn to go home to them for our healing instructions, our liberation maps.

I did a little research on the topic, and it turns out that studies of traumatized mice *and* studies of traumatized holocaust survivor offspring show genetic changes stemming from the trauma.

In the case of the holocaust survivors, a research team at Mount Sinai hospital in New York studied 32 Jewish men and women who had either been interned in Nazi concentration camps, or witnessed or experienced torture. After analyzing their children compared to other Jewish children in families living outside of Europe, those with traumatized lineages were far more likely to have a variety of stress disorders that live in the same part of the brain that controls traumatic activation.

Similarly, in the study with mice, scientists at Emory University asked the question of whether or not one had the ability to inherit a *memory* of trauma. There was one group of mice conditioned to fear the smell of cherry blossoms by pairing their exposure with an electrical shock. Turns out, the offspring of these mice also reacted to the smell of cherry blossoms with fear—even though they'd never smelled them before. On the other hand, the offspring of mice not conditioned to fear cherry blossoms showed no reaction (theguardian.com).

The big beautiful point? Like Myss says, our biography creates our biology. To break the trauma spell, we must go to the root of where it's held. The body—both energetic and physical.

OR PERHAPS THERE'S A SECRET MAGIC HEALER WHO CAN MAKE THIS WHOLE THING A LOT EASIER

Maybe you're reading this chapter thinking that dancing incessantly or 30 days of Bikram is more than you're willing to do to break your trauma spell. Maybe it all feels a bit too scary, or your physiology feels a bit too frozen to move into these kinds of intensities. Maybe you're secretly sitting there wishing there was someone you could simply go to who could undo the deed of your history. Maybe you just want it to be a little more… easeful.

If so, you're about to really love me.

After my major post-surgery mentor-violation fly-back-across-the-country-for-the-fourth-time-in-one-year breaking point, I caved on the DIY healing program and began Googling for the best trauma specialist I could find. A bunch of coaching friends pointed me toward Somatic Experiencing—the modality established by previously mentioned Peter Levine.

Brigit, who I've already mentioned a few times, was my Goddess healing savior. (Though, I'm sure she'd never want me to call her my savior!) Latvian, nearly six feet tall, sturdy boned and sky-blue eyed, she welcomed me into her home office where a massage table sat with four large stones underneath.

I was as terrified as a pound dog, shaky, weary and in desperate need of a caring guide—someone I could trust to not lead me astray. Carefully and quietly, praying this woman wouldn't hurt me, I told Brigit what brought me to her office.

As I told her small bits of my story, she cast her eyes away reverently, offering me deep privacy and personal space. It was something I wasn't used to in the healing industry of tell-everything-off-the-bat, but found truly comforting.

Once I finished talking, nervous, I asked, "So what's next? Should I get on that table?"

"Well, you're actually completely in charge here," she said. "So if you want to get on that table, you can. If you want to stay in this chair, you can. Sometimes clients will sit for the first 30 minutes or however long it takes to simply feel possibly safe in this space together. Whatever you want is what we'll do. And don't worry about time. We have all the time we need."

Huh, I thought. *This is a whole lot of... power... I have here.* Unused to so much permission to control things, so much spaciousness, I took a moment to check in with myself and noticed that no part of me wanted to have anything to do with that table. I wanted to stay in the chair forever. Never move. Just cry.

"I think I'll stay in the chair," I whispered.

"Okay. That's perfect," she responded.

After about two minutes of sitting quietly together, Brigit asked me a seemingly strange question. "So as you're sitting in this chair just now, in this moment, is there anything you notice? In your body... your thoughts... the room around you?"

After telling my story quite quickly, my physiology, unable to handle its rising intensity, spiraled into a freeze state. My mind drew blank. But my eyes—I found my eyes drifting to the four big stones underneath that scary table.

"That brown stone," I said. "I keep looking at it."

"The football-like one?" she asked.

"Yeah, the football-like one."

Brigit let my words linger, let me linger in my words, let the moment linger. There was a *lot* of lingering. After another minute she asked, "Would you like to hold the stone?" My whole body nodded, "yes" so she handed me the football-sized stone and I let it fall to my lap, cradling my womb.

The football stone transmitted so much ancient strength that I was instantly taken aback.

"What do you notice now?" Brigit asked. But I could say no words through my river of tears.

Heat waves moved from my womb, out of my body—up through my chest and face, out the top of my head, then down through my legs, washing clear from my feet. I began to feel like I was no longer on earth. Like time had lapsed and everything was filtered in a chrome-gray light.

"What do you notice now?" she asked again and again and again, as my body moved through waves of experience, flashes of vision, pangs of pain, storms of tears, spirals of shame. As my mind left the space, as I couldn't feel my legs, as my vulva began to scream, as everything built up and boiled over and then finally, *finally*... released, calmed, cradled me.

Before we ever moved to the table, Brigit explained with graphs and chicken scratch the way trauma lives and lingers in the body. She told me that we all have natural blueprints of health, and that if we move slowly enough, with enough awareness and proper guidance, we can click back into our original masterful design—and as we do, as we travel through this slow-fast process of waves, our bodies will release what no longer belongs to us, so long as we allow them to.

I had three sessions with Brigit.

I've since concluded that three sessions with the right witch at the right time can change your life forever.

On our second session, Brigit did some work on my kidneys with her hands, and it began to feel very painful. Eventually, through our slow process of noticing, I asked her to stop touching me—NOW. I'd never used my voice so forcefully. And Brigit complied. Then asked her usual, "What do you notice now?"

"I have the strange urge to become a porcupine with flared quills." I told her.

"That's certainly allowed," she replied.

And so I did. I curled into a ball, flared my back, and in my mind, shot quills as wide as Canada.

Brigit, responding to my threat, moved all the way across the room, stood at the window, and told me my energy had pushed hers all the way outside to the oak tree in the front yard. I'd kept myself safe, she told me, as my body felt like it had fiery rage pulsing out of every pore.

On our third and last session all I remember was that by the end of the 90 minutes, I was pushing Brigit against the wall. My timid, "please don't touch me," upped to a mighty, "Don't Fucking Touch Me," and I knew what it meant to have my voice embodied, protecting me.

What happened in the weeks following was truly the greatest miracle of my life and the impetus for writing this book.

The physiology of my trauma spell... broke. The subtle but pervasive ways that my energy always felt drained halted with immediacy. My "normal" transformed from incessant feelings of hypersensitivity—to people's energies, the volume of the TV, or my own emotionality—to a state of much greater ease and simplicity. I could handle the crowds, because I was operating from my wholeness. The sound of TV still annoyed me, but didn't throw me. My emotions regulated—I could feel them without feeling like they swallowed me. I felt awake, creative, turned on.

I'm sure I sound like an infomercial for traumatic resolution—and that's kind of the point! This is amazing stuff!

The thing I want you to remember is this: you can read, study, or break your mind trying to find the reason why you're so damn stuck. But if you've got trauma, and you want to expel it, travelling to the root of the source will most likely be your greatest help. You can go it alone, or hire a specialist, but the body stores the secret and the body knows how to free it. I'm inviting you to possibly trust it.

KEY 2 QUESTIONS AND PRACTICES:

Take out a piece of paper, and copy these sentence-starters, then fill 'em out, madlibs style:

My body currently craves _____.
My body is hungry for _____.
My body loves _____ more than
_____.
My body hates _____ and needs to stop
_____.
My body is curious about _____.
My body wishes I would _____.
My mind thinks my body should _____ but
my body knows it's time for _____.

"Dialectic Dance" is a fancy phrase for dancing your healing.

Here's the invitation: choose 3 songs. The first song is representative of where you've been—the past that's still alive in you. The second song is representative of where you are now in your journey—how it feels to be exactly in this place and this time. The third song is representative of where you're headed—the you you're growing into, the one who's waiting on the other side.

Choose your three songs and dance them daily or weekly or just fricking once. Dance alone in your kitchen or with a friend or lover as witness. Press record on your video camera if you'd like, or let your movement float into the ether of the walls. Your call. But just dance. And as you dance, let yourself really embody and feel the emotions of each song in the way you move.

Keep a journal near by to record how you feel either during or after your dance. And be really good to yourself when you're finished with this tender, brave practice.

Consider buying yourself a yoni egg. A yoni egg is an egg-shaped crystal designed for healing, strengthening, sensationalizing and cleansing your vagina. You can read through the different kinds of healing energies associated with the different stones and choose the one that feels resonant. Do a little ritual before the first time you insert the egg, praying for healing, vitality, orgasm, forgiveness, pleasure… whatever your yoni is deeply seeking. And be sure you look up instructions about how to properly cleanse your egg before use!

Make yourself a yoni steam. Also known as vaginal steaming or v-steams, a yoni steam is an ancient all-natural healing technique used to cleanse, empower, rejuvenate and beautify your reproductive magic. Do a little googling for how to create your at-home steam, or look for a lovely local practitioner near you.

I'M NOT WILLING TO BE UNCOMFORTABLE FOR YOU

this is the line she told me i need to find
in my mouth, rolling off my tongue
as soon as i've begun to compress

i'm not willing to be uncomfortable for you

strong stranger, aggressive man
quiet seducer, sneaky hands

i'm not willing to be uncomfortable for you

not for your hunger, not for your thirst
this is not about you being put first
not any longer

i'm not willing to be uncomfortable for you
close dancer, space stealer
interrupter, anger wielder
i'm not willing to be uncomfortable for you
not for your dominance

not for your game
not for your desire
to use or to claim

i'm not willing to be uncomfortable for you

not for the point you're trying to prove
that's stacked above the higher truth
that we are *equal* here
you don't get to beat me
there will be no wins at my expense

i'm not willing to be uncomfortable for you

Chapter 7

WHO ARE YOU, REALLY?

KEY 3: REPATTERN YOUR MIND AND SPIRIT FOR NEW WAYS OF THRIVING.

Here's the reason why I encourage body work first (or at least in conjunction with psychological and spiritual processing): once your physiology is more closely aligned to its natural blueprint of health, your reptilian brain has the capacity to calm, and your higher functioning mind can more easily and efficiently... do all that self-help stuff you've been hearing about.

There's a chance that a part of you is sitting there objecting. "But my body was my gateway to BAD, and BAD is what got me into this spiral in the first place. I JUST want to stay in my MIND."

If so, I want you to know I hear you. And... you can stay in your mind for as long as you want. Really. Full permission to stay as far from your embodiment as you desire. You're in charge. I'm not being sarcastic. It's okay.

In the same way that your system has a natural blue-print of health, it also has an inherent treatment plan for when things go awry. It's possible that your inherent treatment plan includes a long, long time staying far, far away from physical embodiment. I will not fight your inherent treatment plan. Your body will tell you when it's ready to be inhabited more fully. I trust that, completely.

In either case—there are powerful opportunities for you in the realm of mind and spirit. Like I said earlier, I did all of these things out of order. There's a magic in the madness, no matter which way you shake it.

TO RENAME IS TO RECLAIM YOUR LOST PARTS

Sex. Sexuality. None of us can avoid it. We're all born of it. And yet, many of us hide from it. Only have it in the shadows. Crave it like a forbidden drug. Or discard it—its power a bit too much (or too terrifying).

Approaching my second Burning Man, I was in deep with questions of sexuality. Dozing off at my bookshelf, I zoomed in on Eve Ensler's autobiography *In the Body of the World* and got fixated with curiosity. (Eve Ensler is most well known for writing viral college campus play, *The Vagina Monologues*.)

Did Eve Ensler change her name? I wondered. *If she didn't, what a destiny!*

Eve—the symbol of the root of all demise. She ate the apple of sin. She decided to defy the bore of immortality and choose the pleasure of NOW, instead.

Thousands of years later, we're all paying for her

pleasure with our fear. Fear of unbridled sex. Shame over saying yes. Aggressive attempts to steal and ravage whatever lust we can get—and then somehow, *please God*, repent.

Eve. Eve. Eve.

I couldn't stop meditating on the symbolism of Eve, so I decided I'd borrow her name at the Burn.

There was something about the way *Eve* felt in my mouth, on my tongue, sharp and strong with sensuality, that even my eyes changed when I said it.

"Hi, I'm *Eve*." and the world dropped back in time.

"Hi, I'm *Eve*." and everyone's genitals tingled.

"Hi, I'm *Eve*." and all anyone could think was, *feed me the pleasure! Just feed it to me. I am not afraid. I do not care if it is poison.*

That year, I was naked 90 percent of the Burn, had the best sex of my life over and over again (physically, emotionally, spiritually), and felt totally alive in my sensual juices. Go figure.

What's the name of your shamed, lost parts, Secret Bad Girl? What's the archetype of the woman you're never supposed to be? Who's the goddess that, god forbid, you might choose to embody—if only for a day, a night in ritual all alone or with girlfriends? I hereby invite you to try her on, give her a whirl.

RELEASING THE LIE OF WOUNDEDNESS AND LESSONS ON SOUL-CONTRACT RENEWAL

The thing is, our bodies can rearrange and open up in strange miraculous new ways, *but*—we still have to be willing to step *into* our newfound aliveness, or inevitably, we regress.

Amidst yet another breakdown in the circuitous sexual trauma cycle, I was talking to Jodi about how alone and misplaced I felt living at home with my parents in the suburbs, doing immense healing work in a non-fitting environment. She listened, and then insisted that I have a session with a new healer she'd met down in Florida.

"Rach. You two will love each other. I know it. She seems super woo woo at first, but she's actually a really smart biologist. And then she also, like, believes in these Pleadian light healing dolphin energy things, and I know it sounds crazy, but she lived in an ashram in India for six years. And... just... I just think you should call her."

"Jo, I like crazy. You know this. What's her name?"

"Star."

"Of course it is. Send me her number."

Star and I met for a Skype session on a sunny spring morning. I told her how living with my parents and the whirlwind of moving back and forth across the country a million times had left me with a sinking feeling that I'd lost my people—that I didn't belong. Not just in terms of place, but also in terms of purpose. And that, in fact, this feeling of not belonging wasn't just as recent as I was making it seem. That somehow, it had been lingering for a long, long time.

Responding with care, Star called in all her energetic supports and began to scan my energy. She sucked in and spit out... entities? Yes, entities. She told me when she saw strange energies, and where, as she invited me to talk about my all-encompassing... problem.

"I just don't feel like I belong here," I told her. "I mean,

I love my parents and all, but they're really not the *healing* types. But the problem is, I don't know where to go."

"Talk to me about the earliest time you had this kind of feeling," Star prompted. I jarred my memory back to life as a kid. Sitting on the couch trying to talk compassion into my parents' shouting matches. Trying and failing.

Star pointed out that it was likely I made a soul contract of sorts when I was a kid in order to stay safe in a violent environment.

"Do you have a sense about what that contract might've been?" she asked.

I felt my heart swell, and the truth spill: "I only belong if I'm wounded."

We took a few deep breaths with it, then went on to do a crazy-cool canceling of the contract. Closing my eyes, with Star's direction, I envisioned my contract written on a scroll. Then watched as I stamped a big red CANCEL on top of it. Out came the paper shredder, and I poured that baby through it. Finally, I sent the remains off to a rainbow flame in the corner of my mind. The whole time, Star read my energies and expelled anything dark or achy. She also had me pull up images of that time—crying on the couch, trying to resolve all the shouts. "Stamp them with the big red CANCEL, Rachael. Send them through the shredder and off to the rainbow flame."

I'm sure I would've thought this was all totally crazy—if it hadn't all felt so damn resonant.

We took a little break, letting the power of what had just happened settle. And then Star asked, "Well… Do you want to write a new contract?"

We bounced ideas back and forth, until finally, it became clear.

"I belong as healed healer."

I cried as we sealed it in, knowing it would change everything.

My family. My sense of place in society and community. My vocation.

And it did. It changed everything. Because what we do to ourselves, we do to the whole. The more comfortable I got with the healed, lit up, alive version of myself—the more my family, friends and work began to reflect the same energy.

As I began expressing my gratitude instead of expressing my resentments, so did my family. As I began making jokes instead of picking fights, dancing with the dogs or exercising and eating right, my parents did more of the same. As I began to own my role as a healed healer—in my work, friendships and world—the more I found myself attracting people who truly appreciated my capacity. No more confusion about my role. No more needing to play small with my power. Everywhere I went, I began to really feel my sense of belonging as a healed healer. It was like the sidewalks glittered in new age gold and all the woo-woo stuff I'd previously made fun of was becoming too powerful and effective to diss.

In addition to the energetic magic, I also worked with an Integral Coach named Chela. A brilliant Canadian woman with a true gift for reading between the lines, Chela helped me identify that I was living inside a Wounded Prodigy archetype. In this archetype, I could swim deep in my artistic emotionality and masterfully analyze things for days. On the other hand, I had a much harder time pursuing that which didn't come naturally, setting boundaries that would uphold my integrity, asking for and receiving my needs, and finding resilience in the face of challenges. (All of these things, by the way, are common themes with people stuck under a trauma spell.)

Chela put me on a program that included the most thorough of bi-weekly inquiries—into power, steadfastness, staying in, reveling in pleasure. She also had me train for a 10k with a walk-run program—one that I had to show up for on the same days of each week, *slowly building into my body* the feeling of consistently expanding my capacity. I met with Chela every two weeks for seven months, and the practice of staying in rather than just piece-mealing my learning was huge in creating a container for sustainable change to take place.

Remember—so much of trauma resolution is about expanding one's capacity to be with intensity—in body, emotion, spirit, and psychology. So whether you're shedding an old soul contract, or stretching into a whole new way of being, if you keep in mind that the goal is to slowly expand your capacity for intensity, you can practice taking small do-able risks towards new, different, bigger, freer, whole. The more consistently you do this, and the more support you get to stay in the practice, the more you'll feel yourself emerging braver and truer in your natural blueprint of health.

KEY 3 QUESTIONS AND PRACTICES:

Who's your "Eve"? The archetype of your inner-self, who's apparently or possibly forbidden or off-limits?

Do you have a story that you can only belong if you're wounded? If that's not quite your hang up, what story are you living inside that's possibly stifling a new story or way of being from coming forth? What feels safe about your current story? What feels excruciating about it? Write it out.

What kinds of healers, coaches or therapists have you been secretly curious about working with? Do you know of someone specific with whom you'd love to work?

What will likely stay the same if you go forth living inside your current story of self? (I know, such a mean question. I love you.) What do you want to shift, in terms of your chronic patterns and belief systems, and why?

DEVOTION

The tongue is the organ of taste, and also the organ of speech, said John O'Donohue.

What is the flavor of the words we don't say?
What is the taste of repression?
What is the sensation of freedom of tongue?

I've watched a thousand butterflies explode
from the back of my throat
out the tips of my teeth
into a quilt of sky and trees

I've felt the gong inside my lungs
the gong of emptiness
the gong of emptied-it-all-out
the rippling quiet joy
And I've tasted the hunger of holding back
the withheld lion claws
waiting for some antelope to surrender—
feed my hollow courage

I've learned there are no martyrs in nature
Who would sacrifice its life, to feed my fear?

I must hunger for the taste of my own depths
I must hunt myself down
puncture my silence
bleed

Chapter 8

YOUR YES. YOUR NO. YOUR HOLINESS.

KEY 4: EMBRACE NEW BOUNDARIES AND SEEK NEW EDGES.

IT'S NOT BAD TO TELL PEOPLE TO FUCK OFF

Shit hit the fan with someone I was dating, and for the first time in my life, a woman friend of mine suggested I block him on social media.

I can do that? I can cut someone out of my life? WHA? I thought. *This guy's nothing compared to the dudes who've raped me.*

That's when I realized I was still Facebook friends with people who'd raped me. Uhhh... Yeah. *No.*

I jarred my memory and searched their names. It felt like a ritual was in store, so I simply made one up. Person by person, I pulled up their page, looked them in the face, and named out loud the energies I was blocking.

TYLER. Addiction. Twice my age. Manipulation. Coercion.

MATT. Addiction. No love. Poly.

JAMES. Abuse of power. Addiction. No love. Twice my age. Secrecy.

HEATHER. Manipulation. Coercion. Secrecy.

MARCUS. Addiction. Coercion. Force.

MONTGOMERY. Abuse of power. Addiction. Twice my age. Secrecy.

Clear patterns emerged, and these blind spots, now brought into the light, became my red flags for bad situations. Upon meeting someone new, I'd ask, *Do they want our relationship to be a secret? Are they twice my age? Are they using manipulative phrases such as "I definitely know what's best for you"? Are they addicts? Are they in positions of power over me?* If so, I did my best to steer clear—but like most change, it took time, and often, I failed at my attempts.

After my surgery I told my good friend Kate that I was thinking about starting to date again. Worried in that heart-full-of-love kinda way, she asked me, *So what are your you-have-to-be-this-tall-to-ride-this-ride rules? You know, the rules of entry?* Here's what I came up with at the time:

1. No sex with addicts.

2. No sex with polyamorous dudes.

3. No sex right away.

While I didn't actually follow those boundaries strictly—I had them, knew them, and knew the risks associated with crossing them. All three of these things were common factors in situations that I'd experience as re-traumatizing or simply shitty, especially while my brain and nervous system were still under the trauma spell.

Having sex with addicts often meant one of a few things: whatever their addiction--pot, alcohol, sex—I'd get roped in. This left me feeling like the sex was ultimately about filling a void or avoiding something deeper, rather than presence and genuine connection.

Having sex with polyamorous dudes often meant lying to myself about what I really wanted—a deeply committed partner to grow and build something with. (Note: this is totally possible in poly relationships, but in my experience is more difficult to cultivate in a monogamy-centered society). I also seemed to be attracting a lot of sex addicts who used poly as a way to feed their addiction. No bueno.

Last, having sex right away generally left me feeling confused, used or attached to the wrong dudes because my hormones were really happy. I wanted to know that whoever my hormones were gonna crave was someone my heart and soul were craving, too. And that it was mutual. So I learned to wait. Horny impatience, and all.

Creating the boundaries for what *wasn't* allowed in meant I had space to start visioning what *was* allowed in—without a bunch of old patterning getting in the way.

And for that, I'll tell you a short story about my awesome friend Shawna.

We're on a walk around a lake in Columbia, Maryland. I'm telling her about my rules of entry, when she quietly smirks and looks over at me. "What?" I ask.

She stops walking. "Okay, so you're focusing on what you don't want—and of course, *that's* what you're attracting. Tell me, in great detail, Rachael, what you'd give a wet-pussied whole-hearted YASSSSS to?"

I bend over in laughter, secretly embarrassed. "I'm not kidding," Shawna says, straight faced. "TELL ME."

"Okay, okay, okay," I say, composing myself. And then I slowly and awkwardly begin to brainstorm the things I could give a whole-hearted, wet-pussied YASSSSSS to.

"A man as brilliant as I am, who's kind and daring and handsome, generously courting me with consistency. A man who takes me dancing. A man who loves to build things. A revolutionary who's rich and wants to give it all back to the earth, together. A man who plays music or paints or makes movies, and wants to do it all to me, on me, with me, in me. A man who's gone to therapy. A man who's excited by my intensity. A man who wants to devour me. A man who insists on honoring me. Our meeting will feel like destiny. We'll both feel more than ready. We'll feel it in our flesh, our bones. We'll know."

I giggled with the truth of what I wanted. What would bring me lively, excited, hungry, voluptuous yeses.

"Nowwww we're talkin'," Shawna laughed. I blushed and smiled all the way to the car.

QUITTING POT. FEELING ALL THE FEELINGS.

A man I was dating introduced me to a mindfulness facilitation teacher who I studied under for nearly 6 months. Every Friday morning, a small group of us training to become facilitators gathered on Google Hangout and entered into an energy vortex of presence. It was powerful, potent stuff. Once the 'field' of presence was created through 30 minutes of meditation and transmission, we'd basically do group therapy for the next hour and a half.

During one of our calls, I was moved to ask for support. Terrified of my fully awakened state (the state in which I'd have to feel just how traumatized I still was), I'd taken to smoking pot pretty regularly.

"I need support quitting pot," I spoke into the circle of mostly-sober spiritual people, all twice my age and ten times as rich. I shrunk to the size of my 12-year-old Bad Girl, but still somehow, I spoke. "I want to come home to myself. I need your help."

That day, I flushed my pot down the toilet. It was a new boundary I was creating with myself. A way to say, *I'm ready to be awake. I'm ready to have faith that it's safe to be awake.*

Practicing this mission of waking all the way up was painful, to say the least. I was forced to feel all my feelings. First and foremost? Just how much I didn't want to be awake. But even though it was highly uncomfortable, it helped. A lot. With access to the truth of my feelings and physical sensations, I was able to meet them fully, and unwind and release them more readily. It's sort of like the saying, *what you resist, persists.* I was no longer resisting. The persistence of my fear loosened. I was better able to simply face the truth: I had some resolution to do. And with time, slowly, I would figure out how, and I would do it.

I want to pause here and just say that lots of Secret Bad Girls have secret addictions that support them. (Mind you, my daily pot habit was definitely *not* public knowledge. *No way.*) For a long time I thought of all addictions as addictions to powerlessness. But now I see them as ways to make our powerlessness more bearable. Because it's truly excruciating to live under the trauma spell—especially since most of us are trying really hard to get out of it, to no avail.

Additionally, substance use has a role to play in the physiology of trauma—it's generally an easy way to soothe and distract into a perceived "safe zone". I'm not telling you this to encourage ongoing substance use—but I am here to destigmatize it. I don't judge or shame myself for my pot addiction (or any addiction you may have). I believe it was part of my inherent treatment plan—a way of calming my nervous system for a while, so I could wake back up when I felt ready. That said, when I was ready to leave the "safe zone" of numb, and enter into the adventure of aliveness, it required a boundary with myself that only love could be strong enough to hold.

These days, with a more regulated nervous system, I smoke pot occasionally. I tell you this because these things are not black and white. What's most important is to ask yourself, *is this bringing me more alive? Is this helping me thrive? What would help me thrive?*

If you remember one thing from this whole book, let it be this: follow your aliveness.

ON THE OTHER HAND, WHAT IF THE DRUGS DO WORK?

So I've shared with you two examples of putting up boundaries—with others, with myself. But sometimes, to get to the other side of something, it actually helps to go *beyond* our comfort zones—shoot the moon, if you will.

The first time I ever tripped on acid I found myself sitting on the dark side of an oversized yin yang swing somewhere near 4 & E at Burning Man. Not coincidentally, Jodi sat across from me in the light.

After a few hours of laughing and enjoying the excitement of the playa, despair started creeping in, until suddenly, I was screaming into the sparkly 3 a.m. sky, "I can forgive my parents for not protecting me! I can forgive that fucker for whatever possessed him to do that to me! I can forgive my poor friend for inviting me into the whole mess! I can even forgive GOD! But I CANNOT FORGIVE *MYSELF*! I was there! I knew what was happening! I CANNOT FORGIVE MYSELF!" (Who cares that I was 13 and wildly manipulated by a 27 year old *and* one of my closest friends at time, right?)

When Jodi needed to take a nap, I went on a solo psychological journey with my terror and the 4 a.m. festival crowds. I stood at the crossroads of 4 & E and asked clearly high bikers if they needed directions. Most were kind and I was able to confidently direct them in some direction (God only knows if it was right or wrong). But one guy got off his bike, and slick and sly, approached me asking if I would give him a kiss. In a terrified child-like voice, I spattered out quickly, "No… umm…. no I will not, sir. This is my little home here. Please… please, now… please go away." After he left I couldn't stop repeating, "I am safe and protected. I am safe and protected. I am safe and protected." It was my beggar's prayer to the playa Gods. Lucky for me, they listened.

That night, more than anything, I was able to see with excruciating clarity just how unhealthy my psyche was. Just how much terror I was carrying in the muscle memory of my flesh. Just how far from safe and protected I truly felt.

The next year, I went on another annual LSD trip to check in on my hidden physiology. I'd done a lot of healing in that 12-month interim, and the night of the big effigy burn, wearing my new name Eve, I found myself undressing completely at the Temple of Grace.

I slung off my white cowgirl boots, my big black fuzzy jacket, the red bandana around my neck, every bit of my jewelry, my bra, my panties—everything—and I humbly prayed to release the past that I still sensed was stuck in my body.

After an hour-long naked meditation just before dawn in which I released imprint after imprint from my holy naked body, a cool breeze blew down my body covering me in a layer of bright white dust. I re-clothed with a sense of deep and mystical calm. I knew there was still a lot to release, but I also knew I was on my way. I would not be stuck forever.

I shot the moon. I got somewhere new.

PERMISSION TO BE ON A MISSION, EVEN IF IT'S A "BAD" ONE

Sometimes, acid breaks you out of your incessant trauma spell and shoots you into a portal of what's possible. Other times, it takes old-fashioned trial and error.

In the years of resolving my sexual trauma, as you've gathered by now, I had a lot of sex. Even though it was often… not so good… I looked at sex as both a mirror and a classroom. How am I doing, now? What am I learning, now? About myself? My body? My psyche? My soul? The way I need to relate in order to feel safe?

I had great sex. Terrible sex. Sex 'til the sun came up. Love making. Lust making. Dissociative sex. Sex with the yoga instructor. Sex without kissing. Sex with women. Baby-making sex. Sex with myself. Sober sex. Stoned sex. Wasted sex. Kinda kinky sex. Sex where I cried "I hate sex" for a full half hour before and after. Sex where I cried "I love you so much" the whole way through, and then practically begged the dude not to leave. Sex with polyamorous people. Sex with multiple people at once. Non-consensual sex. Sex that activated every tingle in my body and blew orgasms out of my ears. Sex with the forest. Sex with the cosmos. I even orgasmed while meditating. More than once.

I learned through trial and error. Mostly a lot of error—and one or two unforgettably love-filled lovers. But it was through this willingness to go farther—in the thick of the bouncing around inside the trauma spell, seeking and finding my raw and realest edges, that I had both some of the best and worst sex of my life. And most importantly—it was during this time that I got really clear on what I wanted more than anything. Devotion. Honesty. Consensual excitement and enthusiasm. Presence. Sobriety. SAFETY. And... love. LOVE. *Love*. Who woulda thought?

Whether you're erecting your boundaries or pushing your edges, remember the very first key (if you can!): move slowly. Build in room to breathe. To regulate. To sit down deep in the center of yourself and wonder, what works about this? What doesn't? What feels holy? What feels like love? What *must must must* I keep?

You get to build your fences of protection and free your secret passion. You get to have it how you like-love-CRAVE it. Truly, Secret Bad Girl. You do.

KEY 4 QUESTIONS AND PRACTICES:

Make a list of all the people you've had violating experiences with. (They don't have to be sexual violations—crappy financial exchanges or a bad deal with a boss work, too… any less-than-ideal exchange of power is great for this exercise.) Next to each of their names, list out the energies or red flag phrases associated with the situation. Then look for commonalities between people. Those commonalities become your red flags…. "No _____" Rules of Entry. Head over to secretbadgirlfreebies.com to get full instructions (plus worksheets) on creating a sacred boundaries ritual.

Once your "no" is clear (and you've cleared a space by declaring it), you've got way more room for your "yes". Ask yourself what Shawna asked me: "Tell me, in great detail, what you'd give a wet-pussied whole-hearted YASSSSS to?"

Are you currently utilizing an addiction of sorts to help cut the edge? If so, what is it? Are you shaming yourself for having it? What's the most loving, compassionate way you can be with yourself, in regards to any addiction you may have? Would you like support quitting or cutting back? If so, what kind of support do you have available to you?

What are the parts of your Secret Bad Girl journey that you've called capital B Bad? With a new context on trauma and the trauma spell, what of those things do you still regret, and what of those things do you better understand? Is there anything you feel compelled to atone or apologize for? Is there anything you feel compelled to forgive yourself for? Write it all out, love. Free your shame.

FUCK ME

i can't wipe clean the image of you and me
fucking, our joy weeps
hummingbird ecstasy
moose bellowing belly glee

i've never been so happy with someone in bed

Chapter 9

THE GREAT EMANCIPATOR

KEY 5: FORGIVE (YOURSELF AND OTHERS)

I'm at Burning Man, 2015—the Carnival of Mirrors. It's my first entry into the Temple of Promise—just about the strangest looking temple I'd ever seen, erected in the shape of an old record-player pavilion, then spiraled like a conch shell with an open-aired center and steel trees in the middle.

I'm dressed in tiny black denim shorts and a strappy black bra with a red bandana swung bandit style around my neck. Dust-covered white tasseled cowgirl boots are protecting my feet from the elements.

It's quiet in that contemplative-temple kind of way. The week has just begun and tiny altars to past loves, parents, pets, and memories are beginning to tack and gather around the wooden two-by-four walls.

I'm taking my time moving through the spiraling structure, breathing in the growing prayers, the empty spaces, the dust dancing in the sunlight that's shooting through the cracks of plywood.

To the right, I notice a crowd of people circled around something out of my sight, each gazing downward with solemn heavy faces.

I mosey over gently and peek my way in, only to see a smallish black chalkboard leaning against the wall. Written in white chalk-paint at the top is a giant *FUCK YOU!*, and underneath, a story. A long, sad story. Of incest. Rape. Violence. With lots of *FUCK YOU*s and I *HOPE YOU ROT IN HELL*s sprinkled in.

I join the circle of witness-readers, frog-throated and churning with grief. Grief and fury and un-phased familiarity.

And then suddenly, the spirit moves me.

I turn around and find a Temple Guardian crouched in all white. She's holding out a black Sharpie marker, hovering it into the open temple air for people like me who've stumbled in unprepared, but with a desperate need to write prayers on those sacred dusty walls.

I bow to receive the Sharpie, give this beautiful woman my eye's kindest smile, and walk back to the black *FUCK YOU!* chalkboard, where I take a deep inhale, belly leaping, then exhale my truth in writing.

I forgive you man (men) who raped me.

I forgive you for your illness & your pain.

I forgive myself for all I never did & also did.

For knowing & not knowing.

Everything belongs.

Rage & rape.
Fury & freedom.
Reclamation & emancipation.
Death & new beginnings.
RIP traumatized vagina.
RIP traumatized soul.
WELCOME WHOLENESS & LOVE.

I don't cry. I'd done plenty of that over the past few years.

Instead, I smile from the pit of equilibrium inside me. I feel strong, like a wizard of sorts, able to rewrite the wires of my past, free myself from the tangles of anger, and stand as a new woman with a new story taking new responsibility for her very new truth.

And for the first time, on this winding road of recovery, I feel like I've finally arrived home. I feel… proud. That I made it out alive. That I found a way to stay dignified. That I could stand so alive and so true.

I can feel people watching me like I'm a living moment of art. Watching me write forgiveness beside *I will never forgive you, you motherfucking fuck*. Watching me scribe acceptance next to, *I hope your soul rots in hell*. And because I'm aware that I'm being watched, and because I'm not actually there for a *righteous* display of forgiveness (uhhh.. fuck that), above the *FUCK YOU!* chalkboard, I scribe an earnest,

I PRAISE YOUR FUCK YOU.

Because I did, and I do.

Because forgiveness isn't something to skip to.

Because the horror of having your honor stolen is riddled with so much self-blame, shame and shut down, that sometimes a wholehearted *FUCK YOU!* is one of the bravest things you can possibly do.

Sometimes we must feel the might of our power before we can soften into the power of our kindness.

Sometimes the kindest thing we can truly do is build an insurmountable boundary of STAY THE FUCK OUT.

Sometimes that's holiness.

Sometimes that's prayer.

Sometimes that's the Secret Bad Girl finally wielding what she's been hiding all along—a fierce sword of wild truth that knows what to do when the world tries to weigh her down with *you're not allowed to want more.*

Sometimes, for a long time, our righteous fight is the most right thing we can use to undo the abuse on our perfectly innocent anger-love-need-lust-longing.

Fuck you, shame monster! Fuck you, aloof mother! Fuck you, perpetrator! Fuck you, cosmetic ad creators! Fuck you, earth desecrators! Fuck you, Frank Allen and Matt Mason and Tornado Sex Guy and Nick Whatever-Your-Last-Name-Is and Mr. Montgomery and suburban boredom and fake religion and genocides of women and a lineage of burning and the bible that lies and the ways we despise the most glorious thing of all: pleasure!

We shout our Fuck Yous! like terrifying hallelujahs, like mesmerizing lion roars, as if underneath all that anger, there's something holy worth fighting for.

Sometimes we have to rage our trauma out until we find the kind of help that teaches us how to unwind from the hell of raging. How to release with gentler pacing. How to not burn and scar ourselves with our own brand of perpetual resentment.

Until we're willing, truly willing, to come all the way into the power of our Secret Bad Girl self who praises, deep down, every acceptable and predictable and wonderful and beautiful and logical and hysterical Bad Girl deed she ever secretly did or wished or wanted or willed into this wildly miraculous yet unprotecting world.

Then. Then we can begin to forgive.

According to Jesus, by way of Caroline Myss, forgiveness is when you agree to not pass on your suffering.

This warrants saying it twice. Forgiveness. Is agreeing. To not pass on. Your suffering.

And so it is, with each wound and wrongdoing, there's a different process for alchemizing the pain without pushing it in the face of the supposed maniacal source. We can be that free, Secret Bad Girls. We can have that much power, that much pleasure, that much will. We can—especially when the time is right, when it's less about fight and more about emancipation.

KEY 5 QUESTIONS AND PRACTICES:

Let's go madlibs all the way through on this one, Secret Bad Girl. Breathe deep. Give it a whirl. And revisit these prompts anytime you feel like you're holding on to suffering extra tight, and a way to ease the pain through words is your core wish. xo

I never *really* let myself get mad or angry about _____.

I've always been afraid that if I let my rage come all the way alive _____ would happen, or worse _____.

_____ is the person I have the hardest time forgiving. I wish they had never _____. Not forgiving feels like _____. I imagine forgiving would feel like _____. What I want the most for _____ [person's name] is _____. What I want the most for myself is _____.

It's also really hard for me to forgive _____ [someone else]. They're not as bad as _____ [first person], but they hurt me in a different way. Again, not forgiving feels like _____. I imagine forgiving would feel like _____. What I want the most for _____ [person's name] is _____. What I want the most for myself is _____. *(Repeat for as many people as necessary.)*

The truth is, there are some things I really can't forgive myself for. _____ is the biggest one. _____, _____, and _____ and close runner ups.

_____ really wasn't that great. I'd like to atone for it by _____.

But _____ really wasn't my fault. If I could just _____ I think I'd feel better about it. I'm going to try _____. That feels brave and loving and good.

Lastly, I'd like to bury _____. Like, really and actually dig a whole in the ground and bury it. I think I'm going to. Is that crazy? Of course not. I'm going to bury _____ on _____ with _____. Wow. That feels… exciting? Liberating. Correct.

One more thing: with all this talk of forgiveness and anger, I don't want to leave out what I'm proud of myself for. _____, _____, and _____ I so often overlook. But really, I'm proud of myself for those things. And actually, _____, too. Even though I wouldn't want anyone to know.

EMANCIPATION

is calling all your orphaned parts home.
We're breaking out of here together, babe.
We're heading for the stars.

Chapter 10

DECLARE IT DONE

KEY 6: REVEL IN YOUR ALIVENESS.

I once took a breathing lesson that was disguised as a voice lesson from a wonderful woman named Awilda. It was post-working with the Brigit-Chela-Star trifecta, and feeling more powerful than ever, I decided I'd go on my very first music tour of original tunes. (As trauma resolves, our daringness expands!) Anyway, I wanted to fuel up with some good voice juju.

Round-faced in the most beautiful way with an adorable grandma pixie cut, a few minutes into our first session Awilda smiled sweetly and asked very Mary Poppinsly, "Now tell me, do you breathe with your vagina?"

Daringness and all, it was still only four months after my vagina surgery and having my lady parts mentioned so forwardly was mucho tender for me.

I started to cry. Then I told her why. (The not so abridged why.)

She sighed the most musical sigh, and pouted with tears of pure empathy—then went on to teach me breathing in the most unbelievable way.

I now use her breathing teaching as a metaphor for how I think of healing nearly everything—but trauma and the Secret Bad Girl Complex, most especially.

Here's the brief of Awilda's instructions:

Inhale, and as you do, allow your breath to move all the way into the back of your skull, beyond your soft palate with your uvula lifted (that little dangly thing in the back of your throat).

Follow your breath all the way down your spine into your lower back, coccyx, and pelvic floor.

Feel your breath fill the entiiiiire well of you.

You've just expanded space for yourself. You've just created deeeeep support for yourself with your breath.

Now... on your exhale, instead of compressing, slouching or dropping down... rather than simply "relaxing", uuuuuse your support and move ooouuutward, iiiinto the space you've created for yourself.

You needn't puuuushhh yourself there. But allow yourself to float! Expaaaaand into the space you've created for yourself.

Maybe you'd like to tilt your head back a bit, spread the wings of your arms back and outward, feel your breasts burning with brand new life.

Feeeeeel your breath supporting your life, then actually expaaand into eeeeven moooore life as you remember to support this expansion with deeeeep back of the body breaths.

Two breaths in, I began to cry.

"This feels... *really* vulnerable."

"Yes, dear," she responded. "This is why people don't actually breathe. To actually breathe is very emotional."

"Okay, that makes sense," I said, as I began surrendering more to my emotion.

"Okay, darling, now inhale again, but this time *speeeak* on your exhale, *voooicing* your expansion."

"What do I say?" I asked timidly, before giving it a try.

"Anything you'd like," she responded with a smile.

"Ummmm... okay." I said stopping, composing myself, then allowing my breathing to fill my deepest well like Awilda had instructed. "Hello... this is my voice, on breath support."

I looked at her awkwardly. It's weird at 28 to re-learn how to breathe and speak. It felt like losing my virginity—my power naked in an innocent kind of truth, my hopes set on someone else approving of all my beauty, knowing it was all in me, feeling strange letting it out.

"Most people never even fill up before they speak," she reminded me. "No wonder it's so hard for us to use the true power of our voices. But now you know, dear, and so now you can SING!"

Again, "Uhhhh... what should I *sing*?!" I spat back nervously.

Again, she consoled me with, "Anything you want, dear."

And then I sang Somewhere Over the Rainbow. Over and over again until I felt like I was that little blue bird flying. It was wildly emotional and excruciatingly vulnerable, but the most amazing thing I'd done in weeks. My heart moved forward in my chest. It bumped up against my ribs. It splintered and splayed at the seams, as if to tell me I could no longer hold in all my love.

"This is wild, Awilda. I feel *so* emotional doing this."

"You should always be able to make yourself cry when you sing," she reassured me. "How else could know that you are truly touching another, if you are not truly touching yourself?"

RIGHT. SOOOOO... WHY'S THE SECRET BAD GIRL GOTTA BREATHE LIKE THIS?

Real simple: after all the healing you do, you don't want to get stuck in a loop of "still wounded". So many people skip this part, afraid of the pleasure of their power, suspicious that they can't be trusted with it when so much bad was done to them by people who misused their authority.

I'm imploring you now: when you're healed, declare it DONE. Resolved. Finished. Over with. And then dare to trust your goodness. Dare to EXPAND into the space you've created for yourself. You are trustworthy. You are decent. You are love. You are discerning. When your new lease on life comes, just accept that you deserve it, you're good enough to enjoy it, and then, for the love of God, move into the house!

When you suddenly feel more sexual appetite than ever before, indulge in sex. When your heart starts to crack open with song, let yourself sing. Daily. As much as heavenly possible. EXPAND into the space you've created with your inhale. Expand, expand, expand.

When your energy levels rise and you feel like you could start a business or a movement or a garden or a band—do it. Use your life force. That's what it's here for.

When your insides rearrange and it's finally the day to say, "I forgive you"—let the words tumble forth. Let the balm of your soothed soul heal people everywhere you go. Let yourself be the light you've been fighting for. Glow. Radiate. Appreciate. Validate. Give it all up. Stuff none of your magic down low.

This is why the *old* you died—to re-birth that original blueprint of magic. Don't regress into a hole of mentally holding yourself back. There's no point in that now. You've changed. You've resolved your old pain. Let your ache be a light ache now—an ache of glorious expansion. You've got the capacity for it. Go for it. You can.

ART IS ALWAYS ALLOWED. –APPLE CAT

Speaking of singing and expanding and re-birth. As a Secret Bad Girl who never thought herself worthy or good enough for her very dearest dreams, I banished myself from the world of music after my junior year in high school. Left it to the domain of my brother, instrumentalist extraordinaire, and my best friend, prodigious indie song-writer. But, *secretly*, I stayed up late writing songs on my baritone ukulele.

After my surgery, which I now know was more like a symbolic death of the old me—after finally working with Brigit and freeing my traumatized physiology, then Chela and Star to unlock my psychology and spirituality—I was no longer that Secret Bad Girl ashamed of her vital sensuality, afraid of the power of her authenticity, insecure and blocked by any attempt to exceed *Wounded* status. While this may sound controversial or maybe even impossible: I was healed. Truly. (Sure, not in all ways, fully, for-evah… I mean, who is?) But things had significantly lightened, opened, expanded. If that's not true healing, I don't know what is.

It was time to let my voice all the way OUT.

"The throat and vagina are energetic mirrors," Awilda reminded me. "As women, we have two mouths. When we allow our song to move through us, it heals us. Cellularly. Completely."

So I sang. I sang through the ache of feeling insanely raw and into the universe of wildly alive. I sang until I could no longer decide I was unworthy of a life filled with beauty. I sang until I knew that God or my natural blueprint of health or my torus or my two year old magic self was always always always within me, always ready to be called on. And still, after that, I kept singing. That music tour was the most fun month of my adult life. Hands down. Expansion crowed me happy. Who woulda thought?

It's my guess that every Secret Bad Girl has her own secret dream of expansion. Perhaps for you, it has more to do with cash or consciousness, embodiment or business. Maybe your most expanded version of self looks like earning a million bucks or living on the land, finishing that yoga teacher training or getting hitched with your dream man or woman. Whatever it is—that thing that calls you all the way awake—you're worth it. It's allowed.

It's your right and your privilege and—dare I say—duty, to embody it. Breathe into it and take the space of it. Go for it. You can.

KEY 6 QUESTIONS AND PRACTICES:

How far have you come on your healing journey? Where have you landed that's good and new? What story, belief, pattern, habit or fear are you ready to declare done? (At least for now, baby.)

What are you ready to EMBRACE? Say yes to? Jump on? Explore? What is your aliveness craving? List it all out. Let yourself move toward your newly accessible yum.

What's the most daring thing you'd let yourself do, if you truly believed you were allowed and good enough to do anything?

YOU, WHO HAS LEFT YOUR COURAGE IN THE SKY

I need you to hear the harrowing scream of our silence.
I need you to listen with your penis.
Listen with your sadness.
Listen with all your ferocious bodily might.
Call home your King.
Call home your courage.
We must rebuild our empire.

Chapter 11

COMING OUT

MOVING INTO THE ALIVENESS MEANS MOVING OUT OF THE STALE SECRET MESS

Habitual. Us humans are habitual. In my own experience, breaking out of the habit of stuckness and expanding into my most alive self was almost as hard as allowing myself to get professional help.

Yes—taking that very first inhale of healing was also fraught with fears. Fears like… *What will happen if I start to breathe? If I start to make space for all the shadows to dislodge and shake their way out? Will I survive? Will it kill me? I think this could definitely kill me.* But the life-or-death fear that was excruciating in the beginning of healing my trauma was quickly replaced with a less physically intense, but still real emotional fear of *not* being stuck. *What will happen if I sing, spread my wings, metaphorically and mythically fly?*

I thought that I only belonged if I was wounded, remember? It takes a lot to change our minds. To uncover and then cellularly integrate that we *belong* as healed healers. That people *want* us and are *actually better off*, when we allow ourselves to thrive in our power. Those people out there may not think so right away. They may feel threatened or abandoned, angry or jealous. But I promise you, Secret Bad Girl, when you're happy, alive and juiced up inside, you become a lighthouse for yourself and others.

We're living in a society that has very little space for true emancipation of the masses with structures of every kind that would crumble instantaneously if enough of us actually woke up. No wonder we stay stuck. Nobody wants to be the wrecking ball. Nobody wants to live inside the rubble. Nobody wants to tear down their cozy shelters to build something better if it means they might freeze to death in the process.

Secret Bad Girls, I hate to tell you this, but we are each architects with the brazen destiny of destroying the false luxuries that are killing us. It's a hard task, but a good one. One that means we get to build homes for future girls—boys, too—who have wild wonderful sex inside them, and who need no good reason to hate or hide it. Instead, our future kids need a thousand safe ways to explore and take pride in their pleasure, their power, their holy blueprints of magic.

The ones of us who wake from our trauma and resolve our personal dramas are the ones who will lead the world into peace. This sounds drastic, but I truly believe it. Trauma resolution means evolving beyond violence and violation. (Not denying or downplaying, but paradigm-fucking. Integrating and absolving and reclaiming and banishing. Whatever it takes to start to feel whole again, to start to renew.)

And because what we do to ourselves, we do to the whole, when we learn how to cleanse and renew our own personhood—our nervous system, our self-hating decisions, our psychological storytelling, our heavy sludge of resentment and mistrust—when we make amends with the traumatic violations of our Secret Bad Girl past, we clear a space in the collective haze for people to awake and follow us.

Look at Oprah, for example—self-described promiscuous teen who was raped as a kid. She's grown into the richest woman in the world, and has devoted her life to being a light-worker and way-finder. Oprah, while not a perfect human, has still undoubtedly broken her trauma spell AND expanded into the fullness of her aliveness. And she's got quite the following waking up with the help of her light.

Look, Secret Bad Girl, the important thing to know is, truly, we don't have to resolve our traumas alone. Hiding in the dark closet of aloneness and secrecy is how we got into this mess in the first place. But now—now we can come out of the shady secret, together. "The master's tools will never dismantle the master's house," as Audre Lorde so famously declared. Let's dive into the sacred destruction together and rebuild something better with all our beautiful, daring hands.

WHAT IF COMING OUT REQUIRES BREAK-ING UP?

Perhaps you're reading the last section, thinking, "Sure, but, uhhhh… What do I do if I was assaulted, raped or molested by someone in my family, close friend group or workplace? My husband? Boyfriend? Partner? How do I 'come out' when the fear is so immense? What if I really really can't afford to ruffle feathers right now?"

My response? I respect your need for safety. 100%. Most people won't ever be as public with their experiences as I've been. Publicity doesn't necessarily mean healing. Sometimes keeping things in confidence feels more healing and reverent to your make up and desires.

Here's a list of 7 ideas for 'coming out' in private:

1)   Write fiction or poetry around the topic and share it with a small writer's group.

2)   Keep an anonymous blog, instagram, tumblr or pintrest account where you share whatever you want—as "extreme" or "emotional" as you'd like—without anyone knowing it's you.

3)   Confide in a confidential therapist, coach or trauma specialist.

4)   Seek a confidential support group.

5)   Get really into vagina any/everything. Post all the time on social media about the pleasure side of the spectrum. Let your outlet be defiant erotic emancipation.

6)   Support a charity that helps fight to end violence against women or human trafficking of girls.

7)   Write a love letter to your younger self, and submit

it anonymously to your local newspaper or a syndicated blog.

On the other hand, you may want to speak up, confront, come out or break the secret seal, but feel unsure as to how. If that's the case, and you're looking for safe and supportive ways to start that journey, here are 3 suggestions:

Who's your absolute safest friend or family member? The person who supports you always and forever, amen? Write them a letter, short or long, detailed or straight to the point, saying the thing you've been keeping a secret. Be sure to also include a sentence or two about how you'd like to be supported by this person. You can either send the letter in the mail, or get together and have them read it with you in person. You also never have to send it, if after writing it, you feel too raw.

Write a letter to whoever violated you. Say everything you ever wanted to say but never did. Send it. Or publish it online leaving out their name. Or burn it like a smoke signal to the Gods, asking for them to help you deliver it. If you end up sending it, be sure you tell at least one good friend or a trusted therapist or coach, and also have a plan in place for buffering a possible response. Are you open to their feedback? Are you closed to their feedback? Decide this before going in, and make it clear in your letter. In the case that you're not open to feedback, phone numbers, email addresses, and all social media accounts can be blocked. If you feel at all like this would be a threat to your safety, please do not go this route.

Conduct a funeral for whatever relationships need

breaking up with. The person who violated you. The person who didn't believe you. The person who broke your trust without apology or remorse. Even if it was your mother, your father, your best friend, your uncle. You're allowed to bury the relationship. Really. A ceremony can symbolically shift things in the material world if you let it. Write a eulogy about everything wonderful and everything terrible. Then write your new declaration of freedom. All the things you're ready to invite in with the burial of this old relationship and violation. Invite your very closest friend or two to bare witness. Buy lots of flowers and funeral food. You deserve them.

Whether you feel ready to 'come out' or keep your secret close is totally your call. And I mean the word call in all the ways. You get to choose—you get to call the shots. *And* if the shots are calling you—if you're hearing over and over and over again that your story needs to be written, or that letter needs to be sent, or your best friend needs to know, or the phone call needs to be made—by all means, hear it as a calling. And call in all the support you can to help make your courage more comfortable. Because 9 times out of 10, these things are *not* comfortable. But they can be revolutionary—if they're truly calling. Listen deep. Respond to the truth inside you.

BRIDGES

Jodi taught me about bridges
the other day after dance

to move from scarcity
to sufficiency

you appreciate
what you have

to move from sufficiency
to prosperity

you ask for what you want
and know when to walk away

tonight Chris suited back up after we made love
black jeans, belt, tucked in shirt, sturdy boots
I laid naked in my white jersey sheets
and watched him walk away

Chapter 12

WHEN COURAGE CALLS

A few weeks before I began writing this book, I was invited to a sacred cacao ceremony with a Guatemalan shaman in Harper's Ferry, West Virginia. I arrived to Healer's House at the top of a mountain overlooking the Shenandoah River just as the sun was setting, turning all the autumn leaves to bronzes and golds.

That night, a round older indigenous man from Guatemala and an almost-albino young white woman led 10 of us in an ancient cacao ceremony where we drank a potent chocolate medicine and sang and drummed around a fire in the woods. I'd partaken in cacao ceremonies before—where the rawest and purest chocolate is made into a potent drink that heightens your state of awareness—but none like this one. The drink was four times as strong as usual and I drank at least four times as much of it. My heart was the size of Mars, and hot.

When we got back down to Healer's House, everyone began to feel sick. A few people vomited. Most cried. The guides came around and did acupressure on our hands, spoke to our souls, wafted essential oils under our noses. But there was nothing—nothing—anyone could do to slow my deluge of tears.

They asked me what I was thinking, but I could barely breathe, let alone speak. I just thought my deepest truth: I'm lonely. I'm tired of the fight I've been carrying, tired of being so strong on my own, tired of Keeping It Together. I'm ready for holy love. Or at least a bit more lightness.

Eventually, after being enveloped in a three-way hug for a good thirty minutes, I began to feel like maybe I could rest.

We all moved to our respective sleeping bags and the room filled with a lullaby of snores, except now there was a familiar excruciating pain rising up and throbbing throughout my whole right vulva. And now, there was a river of fury moving through me that nothing could dam or dismiss. And now, there was a spiral of insanity. And now, I could not stay in that sleeping bag, pretending to be sleeping sweetly. No fucking way.

I got up, grabbed my phone, slipped someone else's small red clogs onto my ice cold feet, snuck out the side door, and made my way through wet grass and pummeling rain into the driver's seat of my car. With my vulva still on fire with pain, I closed the door and wailed as hard and loud as the pounding rain on my windshield, hoping, praying, begging that SOMETHING would wash the ache out.

My prayers were not being answered, so I figured it was an appropriate time to phone a friend. No matter that it was 2:30 a.m. *They'll think it's an emergency, and answer*, I thought. *This IS an emergency*, I rebutted in my own head.

I called Jodi on the west coast. No answer. I called Jen on the east coast. No answer. I called John Damien and Justin and Chris and even Karen. No answer. No answer. No answer. None. None of my emotional emergency contacts were answering. So I did what every not-sober person does late at night, lonely and desperate with an aching vagina. I began scrolling my contact list. Finally, I came across a name I was surprised to see. Matt Mason. The guy with his own war PTSD who date raped me just after my divorce.

I let my finger hover above his name. Clicked on the contact. And then without a second thought, said *fuck it*, and called.

On the third ring, he answered.

"Oh…hi! Matt. It's Rachael Maddox. You're up! Or did I wake you?"

"Ummm. You woke me. But that's okay. What's up?"

And then I blubbered out my practical whole life story as shortly as humanly possible.

"Well… uhhh… I had this big cancer scare a few months ago and had to have surgery on my vagina, and now I'm really afraid that I might have something like cancer again because my vagina really hurts, and so I'm just trying to let go of anything that might possibly be stuck in me. And… uhhh… you know that night when I came over and we had sex? Yeah. That night wasn't okay. And I'm not here to yell at you or even get mad or anything. I just want you to know that you said some things… things like, *What--you're not used to being fucked like this* as you kinda *really* railed into me… and then I was really not okay… and then I woke up in the fetal position in the corner of your bed with tears on my face… And, yeah… I just want to let it all go."

"Wow," he stumbled. "Well.. uhh.. sounds like you're going through a lot. I don't exactly remember it that way, but that's okay."

"Ummm… well, yeah… I do. And… it's been really… a really hard few years."

"Okay, well I'm sorry you're having a hard time. I really am. I don't usually get calls like this."

We bumbled back and forth a little bit more, and then I simply said it. "Look, not that you're asking for it, but I forgive you. That's all I wanted to say."

"Okay. Well, thanks. Be well, Rachael. I'm going back to bed."

We hung up the phone and my body exploded like a great volcano that had been waiting for ages to erupt. For minutes hot sweat, steaming energy and bundles of tears fled out of me, until finally there were nothing left but a radical quiet calm, and I watched the raindrops chase each other down my windshield.

"Huh!," I said out loud to myself. "That felt… *good*."

Immediately my mind went to Heather. I needed to call Heather.

I texted Micayla, *Do you have Heather's number?* She texted back right away.

The next day I got up feeling dazed and wanting to

quietly escape without saying goodbye. I drove to where the Shenandoah River met the Potomac, parked my car and walked to the confluence. Two young girls, maybe eight years old, were playing together at a tiny shore. A man was fishing in tall boots. Tourists with big cameras were capturing the autumn foliage. I floated around until I found a cluster of large rocks gathered together like a family. I climbed over one to sit atop another with my legs dangling in mid air. I watched the water dance slowly over the rocks, gentle ripples going exactly where they needed to go.

I'd never once considered that calling Heather was an option—something that could be part of my healing. I didn't even consciously realize I'd been harboring any aggression against her. But that day, there was no anger or regret. No blame, fear or malice. Just a body that housed a deeply good soul, sitting cradled between a few great mama rocks, with a kind and gentle river below.

I made no plans, recited no speeches. I just picked up the phone and called, the way you might call a long lost relative, knowing—trusting—that even after all that time, you'd still be family.

Heather and I talked for forty-five minutes.

"Do you remember that night?" I asked.

"It's haunted me all my life," she confessed.

And she told me the whole story from her horrendous aching vantage point. The compassion between us was unnumbered, and as I listened carefully to her, a new secret story revealed itself. Heather and I were both Secret Bad Girls, grown up fat girls, a bit more adventurous than the average girls, smart but over-pleasing girls. We were the

177

same prototype of hidden wild magic delight with nowhere appropriate to give or receive our love. We were trauma, all grown up, in a society that expected nothing more from us. The only difference between us was I had given the last decade of my life to resolving the strife I somehow knew was not actually mine. She, on the other hand, was still trying to make peace with it all.

We hung up the phone, and a half hour later, she sent me this text:

Just wanted to thank you again for your courage to call me. Although I don't feel like all of the weight has been lifted off my chest (I have to deal w/ personal stuff before that happens), I certainly feel renewed and am so grateful for your call. You have been and always will be a healer – I hope you stay well and continue to heal and grow yourself.

At that moment, I looked up and saw those two girls splashing in the river. I knew it was time to write a book— for Heather, and for all the Secret Bad Girls who are still sitting in the shadows of their shame. A book as if to say, What if there's a different way? What if it wasn't your fault? What if it doesn't have to be so difficult? What if you're one of billions? What if you've been spiraling under a spell that's possible to break? What if what it takes won't actually re-traumatize you, because people have gone before you, spent decades of their life flailing and fumbling, only to finally find their way above water with a message loud and fearless: you can do this. You can rewire your cellular history. You can rewrite your fraught psychology. You can loosen your grip on rage after you've let it ripple safely through your caged up flesh, and then—then you can dance the freedom in. You can have your impossible dreams. You can begin a whole new book.

I pictured those girls growing up in a world ravishing and on fire with their desire, with nothing wrong, nothing to unarm, places to play and ways to stay safe as they learned how to make magic from their holy innocent powerful lusting love. Maybe they're good. Maybe they're bad. Maybe they're all of it, and there's nothing wrong with any of it.

About the Author

Rachael Maddox is a trauma resolution educator, coach and guide who's helped hundreds of women and men resolve their sexual trauma and reclaim their pleasure, power and wholeness through one-on-one support, groups, courses, trainings and educational material on all things sexual healing and whole-life reclamation.

Rachael is best known for her multi-pronged approach to healing and reclamation that includes sound physiological context, embodied scientific research, pleasure as a super power and magic as medicine.

Rachael's professional training includes Alchemical Alignment Trauma Resolution & Embodiment of Spirit, The Coaches Training Institute and The Awakened Leadership Academy.

For fun, Rachael writes songs on her ukulele, swims naked as often as possible, and lays quietly under trees.

You can find more information about studying or working with Rachael at rachaelmaddox.com.

Acknowledgements

This book would not be possible without the village that helped me raise it. To Jen, for being the first person to ever tell me it wasn't okay what happened to me, for mentoring me at every turn, and for sending me to Angela when the time was just right. To Angela, for knowing and honing the craft of creation, and to Mila for pulling me through to the end. I love you each to the moon and back.

To my inner circle of friends and family who generously supported my publishing process at the very beginning, I love you: Tina and Kim, Mikey, Uncle Barry and Aunt Micale, Karen, Micayla, Mom, Dad, Jodi, Stacey, Justin, Kate—thank you for being with me all this time, and for leaping with me when I needed you the most.

To Jeanette for flying in like the most exquisite angel-doula to help me push the baby out, and to the 234 Kickstarter backers who brought it all the way to the finish line! I love you! Your support and enthusiasm gave me so much courage and strength: Rebecca, Dr. Rachel, Mara, Elizabeth, Nicholas, Jeremy, Nona, Lola, Kristina, Alex, Randy, j, Kelly, The Grey, Corinna, Francie, AGJ, Nicoletta, Shannon, Rachel, Shane, Alaya, Molly, James, Kimi, John, Iman, Jane, Diane, Torie, Brian, Jodi, Gabriella, Paula, Jenna, Janis, Naima, Lionessa, Britte, Pamela, Krista, TaRessa, Melissa, Dave and Roxy, Liz, Alexis, Rachel, Don, Lara, Molly, Heidi, Carol, Russell, Ann, Beth, Alex, Allie, Laura, Shannon, Vanessa, Laurie, David, Caroline, Jessica, Mia, Lisa, Nicci, Elissa, Elaine, Cindy,

Ian, Anne, Reise, Julia, Melinda, Jessica, Devon, Chela, Jeanette, Rachael, Megan, Lindsay, Luna, Carolina, Karen, Jacqueline, Sharlene, Katie, Rasa, Danielle, Laurie, Ria, Sara, Jeff, Mary, Ashley, Christopher, Maribet, Jenni, Aleece, Neall, Judy, Madeline, Garrett, Marion, Micayla, Rachel, Whitney, Tim, Tulasi, Karen, Dean, Emma, Melissa, Alyson, Haley, Carissa, Paul, Valerie, Len, Kyeli, Sara, Tricia, Katie, Sacha, Adriana, Karen, Julie, Chenoa, Shamar, Heather, Casey, Joyelle, Devra, Katie, Sarah, Kim, Amy, Winona, Rachelle, Danielle, Kimberlie, Jessamyn, Shila, Karen, Andrea, Carena, Tracy, Tessa, Nadia, Stephanie, Marija, Anthony, Holly, Max, Shelly, Jill, Amy, Miriam, Debbie, Vegan, Kristen, Heidi, Terri, Alyssa, Chana, Trisha, Dan, Brianna, Laura, Meryl, Lacey, Jen, Sarah, Scarfy Matt, Meg, Rose, Amber, Jeanne, Skaja, Sara, Jackie, Meghan, Jamie, Brooklyn, Kate, Anthony, Lacey, Leigh, Jen, Amy, Raakhee, Christel, Anna, Mary, Alexander, Johannes, Marissa, Mandy, Lizzie, Stephie, Andy, Melissa, Caroline, Paige, Tenkai, Darrah, Sandee, Shawna, Sarah, Nawal, Jazmyn, Stacy, Benjahmin, Stephen, Fiona, Toby, Tracey, Laura, Gina, Allison, Nina, Anu, Helen, Meg, Serenity, Danielle, Mary Ann, Beverly, Mike, Valerie, Dawn, and Darrell. HOLY YES, THANK YOU.

To Heather, for the invitation to be bad. I love you. I believe in you. I forgive you. To Matt, for a soul contrarian courtship like no other. Bless your broken soul. May everything healing come to you.

To Brigit for working true miracles with her hands and heart. This would've been so much harder without you. To Melissa, Awilda, Lola, Chela and Star—for heal-

184

ing and guiding me back to wholeness. You are each such endless blessings. Thank you for all the work you've done on yourselves to be able to offer such immense, refined gifts of love.

To the Portland ecstatic dance community for being a terrifyingly safe and transformative playground. Bless your sweaty wild souls.

To Peter Levine, Eve Ensler, Audre Lorde and Naomi Wolf for the cannon of brilliance that inspired, taught and comforted me in the dark. I forever recommend you.

To my inner-circle of soul sisters who encouraged me at every turn: Judy, Molly, Kate, Valerie and Paula. Every ounce of "you can do this," "people need this," and "keep going" I swallowed like holy medicine. Thank you, thank you, thank you. And to Jodi for 10,000 hours of endless listening, deepening, knowing and seeing. This book would've never happened without your unending faith in me. You are such an angel. Thank you.

Michael, thanks for believing in my power in quiet committed ways. Dad, you are unwaveringly fair, enthusiastic and supportive. Mom, you are resilient, understanding and pure true love. I'm so glad we all chose to be family. Your consistent patience with and faith in me were the bedrock upon which I could build this book. Thank you. I love you. Forever and ever, amen.

Additional Resources

Moving through this territory alone can be super challenging. Here are a handful of trusted and reliable resources that may support you in your process.

secretbadgirlfreebies.com has a toolkit with a healing meditation, boundaries ritual, trauma 101 and more.

ReBloom, Rachael's second book, and the accompanying Workbook, is a thorough resource of stories, strategies and exercises for healing from the worst of it and emerging as a pleasure-filled and powerful new you.

rachaelmaddox.com has many opportunities for healing or studying with Rachael, either in groups or one-on-one.

traumahealing.org is the homepage for Somatic Experiencing (founded by Dr. Peter Levine) that has a feature where you can search worldwide for a local practitioner near you.

traumasensitiveyoga.com is the homepage for the Trauma Center's Trauma Sensitive Yoga (founded by Dr. Bessel van der Kolk) that has a feature where you can search worldwide for a local teacher near you.

alchemicalalignment.com is the homepage for the Alchemical Alignment practitioner training (founded and taught by Brigit Viksnins). Brigit's teachings are life-changing and I couldn't recommend them more.

centers.rainn.org is the homepage for RAINN (Rape, Abuse & Incest National Network) – the US's largest anti-sexual violence organization – that has local hotline numbers, tons of educational resources, and vast directories for finding professional support near you.

21708426R00106

Made in the USA
Middletown, DE
13 December 2018